FINDING YOUR BALANCE

Personal and Professional
Wellness Strategies
for Effective
Educational Leadership

JOSHUA RAY

Foreword by Mike Mattos

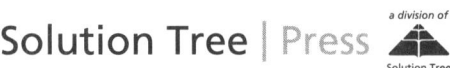

Copyright © 2025 by Solution Tree Press

Materials appearing here are copyrighted. With one exception, all rights are reserved. Readers may reproduce only those pages marked "Reproducible." Otherwise, no part of this book may be reproduced or transmitted in any form or by any means (electronic, photocopying, recording, or otherwise) without prior written permission of the publisher.

555 North Morton Street
Bloomington, IN 47404
800.733.6786 (toll free) / 812.336.7700
FAX: 812.336.7790

email: info@SolutionTree.com
SolutionTree.com

Visit **go.SolutionTree.com/educatorwellness** to download the free reproducibles in this book.

Printed in the United States of America

LCCN: 2024046473

Solution Tree
Jeffrey C. Jones, CEO
Edmund M. Ackerman, President

Solution Tree Press
President and Publisher: Douglas M. Rife
Associate Publishers: Todd Brakke and Kendra Slayton
Editorial Director: Laurel Hecker
Art Director: Rian Anderson
Copy Chief: Jessi Finn
Senior Production Editor: Christine Hood
Proofreader: Sarah Ludwig
Text and Cover Designer: Rian Anderson
Acquisitions Editors: Carol Collins and Hilary Goff
Content Development Specialist: Amy Rubenstein
Associate Editors: Sarah Ludwig and Elijah Oates
Editorial Assistant: Madison Chartier

Acknowledgments

Throughout my career in educational leadership, a handful of people have helped me be the best version of myself. If not for each of them, I would have surely failed, and you certainly would not be reading this book. First and foremost, I want to thank the love of my life, my wife, Sarah. Regardless of what life throws my way, I have never once been alone. She is my cheerleader, my supporter, and the swift kick in the pants I regularly need. I don't know how I could have possibly deserved such a partner, but I am who I am today because of her. Our sons, Hudson and Harrison, push me to be my best as a man and an educator. Nothing makes me as happy as being a dad. Not a day goes by when I am not incredibly proud to be their father. Of the titles or positions I've held, none makes me as proud as being Sarah's husband or Hudson and Harrison's dad.

The older I get, the more I recognize just how lucky I was as a child. My parents, Jesse and Tammy Ray, are the most giving, selfless human beings I have ever known. They spent their entire lives building a life for my brother and me that was better than their own. Throughout my career, the sweet, caring support of my mother and the belief and encouragement of my father became the models for who I aspired to be for my students. Of the many gifts they gave me, none are as precious as my brother, Jacob. He is a man of great character, an inspiration, and an unwavering support in times of need.

As important as family is, there are others without whom this book would not exist. While they may not be blood relatives, they have become family in their own right. Faith Short is the sister I never had. At my most infant state of leadership, I found strength in her incredible skill set. Instead of wondering why her district chose a band director to be her new principal, she invested in me, pushed me, and helped me be the leader I could have never been on my own. So much of my success in leading others began with the friendship we built working together. Stephanie Griffith, Ashley Richey, Becky Chatman, and Brandon Tate completed our leadership family in my first school. These people saw me at my worst and helped grow me to my best.

In the pages that follow, I'll talk a lot about Aaron Gamble, my best friend, whose life was cut tragically short along with his son's. I want to thank Tara Gamble and Dacie Gamble-Dunn. I'm not sure I have ever met stronger human beings. The brotherhood I shared with Aaron Gamble changed the course of my life. While I can share the stories of our friendship, Aaron and his son Landry belonged to them. For Aaron, the sun rose and set on his lovely wife, Tara. She was the strength behind the man who inspired many. Also, as a former mathematics teacher himself, Aaron couldn't help but gush about his daughter, Dacie, who followed in his footsteps. I wish so badly he could have been there when she received a perfect score on her mathematics teacher certification exam or when she was hired to teach mathematics in the very building he once led. When I think about Aaron, his wife, and his daughter, I can't help but remember something my dad once told me as a young man: "Behind every great man is a better woman." I'm not sure there is a better example of this than Aaron and the incredible women he loved most.

After the loss of my best friend, the weight of assuming the role of high school principal could have crushed me. Amanda Maxwell, Chase Meyers, Travis Sandifer, and Christy Hesslen helped me lead through tragedy. The friendships we built through some of the most challenging days of our lives are treasures I'll cherish forever.

While I owe so much to my family and friends, this book would not be possible without the incredible publishing team at Solution Tree. I want to thank Douglas Rife for publishing this book and giving me the opportunity to help other leaders. Claudia Wheatley has become my dear friend and mentor. She pushes me to be my best and champions my work. Finally, Amy Rubenstein and Christine Hood took the rambling thoughts of an educational leader and polished them into something worthy of publication.

Solution Tree Press would like to thank the following reviewers:

Taylor Bronowicz
Sixth-Grade Mathematics Teacher
Albertville Intermediate School
Albertville, Alabama

Courtney Burdick
Apprenticeship Mentor Teacher
Fort Smith Public Schools
Fort Smith, Arkansas

Carrie Cutler
Clinical Associate Professor
University of Houston
Houston, Texas

Janet Gilbert
Principal
Mountain Shadows Elementary School
Glendale, Arizona

Kelly Hilliard
GATE Mathematics Instructor NBCT
Darrell C. Swope Middle School
Reno, Nevada

Teresa Kinley
Humanities Teacher
Calgary, Alberta, Canada

Acknowledgments

Erin Kruckenberg
Fifth-Grade Teacher
Jefferson Elementary School
Harvard, Illinois

Vanessa Cevallos Reyes
Principal
Sam Rayburn High School
Pasadena, Texas

Janel Ross
Principal
White River School District
Buckley, Washington

Lauren Smith
Instructional Coach
Noble Crossing Elementary School
Noblesville, Indiana

Rosemarie Nodine Swallow
Social Studies Teacher
Lava Ridge Intermediate
Santa Clara, Utah

Visit **go.SolutionTree.com/educatorwellness**
to download the free reproducibles in this book.

Table of Contents

ABOUT THE AUTHOR xi

FOREWORD xiii

INTRODUCTION 1
    The Journey to Wellness 2
    In This Book 4

CHAPTER 1
Balancing Work and Life 7
    About Balance 11
    Who Becomes an Educational Leader 12
    The Stages of Leadership Imbalance 14
    Imbalance Versus Balance 19
    Strategies to Help You Find Balance 26
    Conclusion 30

CHAPTER 2
Making Time for Physical Wellness 31
    About Physical Wellness 32
    Physical Wellness and Decision Making 35
    Physical Wellness as a Priority 43
    Strategies to Improve Physical Wellness 45
    Conclusion 50

CHAPTER 3
Being the Leader You Aspire to Be 51
    About Being the Leader You Aspire to Be 52
    Leadership Traits and Styles 53
    The Pursuit of Happiness 55
    Leadership Self-Assessment 56
    Leadership and Time Priorities 59
    Strength-Based Leadership 61
    Strategies to Manage Your Time 62
    Conclusion 65

CHAPTER 4
Leading Change 67
    About Leading Change 70
    The Lippitt-Knoster Model for Change 71
    Rational and Irrational Resistance to Change 74
    A Structure for Healthy School Accountability 80
    Strategies to Diagnose, Understand, and Address
        Resistance to Change 83
    Conclusion 89

CHAPTER 5
Sharing Leadership 91
    About Sharing Leadership 93
    How to Lead Your Leaders 99
    Strategies to Build Shared Leadership 102
    Conclusion 109

EPILOGUE
Putting It All Together 111
    Know the Five Fundamental Truths of Leadership 111
    Share Your Story 113

REFERENCES AND RESOURCES 115

INDEX 121

About the Author

Joshua Ray, EdD, is an educational speaker and author who has led the Professional Learning Community at Work® (PLC at Work) process at the elementary, secondary, and district level. He is passionate about building healthy school cultures, the work of collaborative teams, systems of supports for students, and educator well-being.

As assistant superintendent, Dr. Ray helped schools collaboratively build district common assessments, unite around common expectations, and improve teaching and learning. He worked alongside principals and instructional coaches to make the PLC at Work process practical and meaningful in the everyday life of their schools.

Prior to being named assistant superintendent, Dr. Ray was principal at Greenwood High School and East Pointe Elementary School. Under his leadership, both campuses were selected by the Arkansas Department of Education to participate in the Arkansas PLC at Work project. Because of the impact of the PLC at Work process, Greenwood High School became a destination for schools and educators across the state looking to learn how to implement this work on secondary campuses.

Similarly, East Pointe Elementary went from a "B" school to a distinguished Arkansas campus in the top 5 percent of performance and growth, resulting in nearly $150,000 of reward funding from the state of Arkansas. For their work in the development of student leadership and agency, East Pointe was nationally recognized as a "Leader in Me Lighthouse School" by Franklin Covey.

Outside of his district, Dr. Ray serves as a member of Arkansas's state guiding coalition focused on developing PLCs throughout the state. He also serves as an adjunct professor at the University of Arkansas.

As a researcher, Dr. Ray was chosen to represent the University of Arkansas at the American Educational Research Association Conference as a David L. Clark scholar for his work on the wellness practices of educational leaders. He has published research on PLCs and educator well-being in *Principal Magazine*, *The Standard*, *AllThingsPLC Magazine*, and the *Journal of Educational Administration*. These scholarly endeavors have provided him the opportunity to present throughout the United States and Canada.

During his time in the classroom, Dr. Ray was a Phi Beta Mu inductee, designated as Arkansas's outstanding young band director, and awarded the National Band Association's Blue Ribbon Designation for his work as a music educator.

Dr. Ray holds a doctorate in educational leadership from the University of Arkansas. He is a National Board Certified Teacher and an Arkansas Master Principal graduate.

To learn more about Dr. Ray's work, follow him @JoshRay711 on X.

To book Joshua Ray for professional development, contact pd@SolutionTree.com.

Foreword

By Mike Mattos

As educators, what we do matters. Our profession has the distinct privilege—and the awesome responsibility—to develop and nurture human potential. We ensure students learn the essential academic skills, knowledge, and dispositions needed for lifelong success. We prepare future citizens and open doors of endless possibilities for our students. Our work echoes for generations to come.

I believe most educators join our profession for exactly this reason . . . because what we do matters. It is why we frequently work beyond our contractual hours, regularly spend our own money on work supplies, and often neglect our personal needs. Educators' nightmares are often the reoccurring dream of being in front of students ill-prepared and under ludicrous conditions. We worry about students, past and present, who we failed to reach. If our work was redundant or inconsequential, we would never willingly sacrifice so much.

And because our work matters, the payoff for investing so much is hopefully greater than our monthly paychecks and retirement benefits—that moment when you see a struggling student finally grasp a new concept, and you see in their eyes that sense of self-efficacy and accomplishment. Or perhaps a past student finds you on social media—years after they left your class—to share that you made a difference. These moments are priceless. But like a high-stakes poker game, if we do not play the game skillfully and intentionally, we can lose ourselves and end up professionally and personally bankrupt.

I spent twenty-two years as a site educator; the first twelve years as a classroom teacher. I vividly remember specific students with behavioral needs that made almost every teaching day a challenge. On numerous occasions, I was legally bound to report suspected child abuse, with one parent confronting me in the parking lot for contacting child-protective services after his daughter confided in me that her bruises were caused by a parent angrily throwing her down a flight of stairs. I distinctly remember specific students that did almost nothing in my class. Regardless of how many ways I tried to connect with each of them, they slowly slipped deeper and deeper below grade-level in my class. And I have regrets that my pedagogy skills in my first several years of teaching were lacking for students who were not fluent in English. Don't get me wrong; I also have many extremely positive and rewarding memories from my classroom years. But because our work matters, the sting left from my struggles often weigh harder on my conscience than the warmth felt from my successes.

When I left the classroom for an administrative position, I naively assumed that my dozen years in "the trenches" of education had properly prepared me for the job ahead. I could not have been more wrong. The challenges I faced as a classroom teacher were exponentially greater when I was assigned my first principalship. Every challenging behavior student in the school was now my student. Every serious parental problem ended up on my desk. Every disengaged and struggling student was my concern. Every English learner depended on my instructional leadership.

In addition to feeling the weight of every student's success, I had new responsibilities I never faced as a classroom teacher. I was responsible for the hiring, evaluation, and retention of teachers and support staff. For anyone who has ever had to fire a staff member—and potentially end someone's career—it is an incredibly important and painful responsibility. Determining teacher assignments, navigating staff disagreements, and leading difficult change processes are fraught with stressful days and restless nights of reflection.

I remember driving to work one February morning during my first year as a principal and feeling dread when I saw the freeway offramp for the school. For the first time in my career, I feared that I had wagered too much and had nothing left to give. I know what saved me that year was the tremendous love and patience of my wife, because I know I would have never weathered that storm alone.

These honest reflections are not intended to scare you away from being a leader or to suggest that your best way to deal with the inevitable stresses of the job is to hope for an unreasonable level of personal support from loved ones in your life. My point is this: Nothing in my master's program in school administration remotely prepared me to successfully navigate the innate challenges of leadership. In fact, the topic was never acknowledged, let alone proactively addressed.

Fortunately, there are proven ways to find the necessary balance between the demands of your professional work and your personal needs. The very purpose of this outstanding book is to develop your leadership skills while protecting your physical, mental, and emotional health!

The author of this book, Joshua Ray, is an awarding-winning administrator and a nationally recognized expert in professional learning communities. His advice and recommendations are based on research, honed in the field, and validated with results. He has personally faced the challenges of leadership and offers practical solutions. Most importantly, he understands that our work matters, but so do the educators who serve our students.

I sincerely thank you for accepting the challenge of leadership. While I shared some of the challenges of the work, I don't regret for a single second my decision to join our profession. I can think of nothing more rewarding than to make it your life's work to help students reach their fullest potential. What I do regret is that this excellent resource was not available when I started my own leadership journey.

Introduction

I couldn't help but feel excited at the end of the day. I was far from home but still feeling the exhilaration of a day of professional learning with a great group of teachers. If I was honest with myself, I still couldn't shake the feeling of how strange it felt that they would want to learn from me. I was incredibly lucky, for both the experiences that brought me to this moment and the chance to help others around the country. I began packing my backpack and was already thinking about my traditional call with my wife and boys on the way to the airport.

In that moment, there was an awkward sound, like a person clearing their throat. I looked up to see the principal of the school standing alone, waiting for me. Dressed in a perfectly pressed suit and presenting herself with poise and professionalism, she impressed me all day with her questions and presence with her staff. I had nearly forgotten to check in with her, as she quickly left the room when our day ended. "Do you have a little time to visit before you leave?" she asked. All the strength she portrayed during our day together had seemed to disappear, leaving only a slight, almost childlike, trembling voice. "Of course," I said and began following her throughout the building.

I began to question if the day had gone as well as I had originally thought. She had seemed so engaged, and I felt like her staff really learned a lot. But suddenly, I couldn't shake the feeling that I had done something wrong. We walked into a large office, which was meticulously organized. She dropped into a large leather chair behind an imposing desk. Everything around her seemed to portray power and confidence, which stood in stark contrast to the broken figure of the leader in front of me, her head hung haphazardly in what could only be interpreted as defeat. I watched as two tears dropped from her face to form circles on the large, detailed desk calendar in the center of her desk. It was likely less than two or three minutes, but after what felt like a lifetime later, she raised her head to reveal two watery, red eyes. "I don't know if I can do this," she admitted and immediately dropped her head into her hands and continued to cry.

Stunned by the turn of events and unsure of what to say, I couldn't help but notice the credentials hanging above her head. Four degrees, a certificate for teacher of the year, a national board teaching certification, and a key to the city all presented the picture of a strong, confident young leader. However, in front of me was a broken young woman who seemed embarrassed. After a moment, as if reminded of who she was supposed to be, she regained her composure, wiping her eyes and apologizing for her outburst.

She explained that over the course of the day, she couldn't shake the feeling that everything we were talking about was great for their school, but she wasn't sure she was good enough to lead it. Thankfully, I had the chance to share my story with this young leader to encourage her and build a professional partnership that continues to this day.

My drive to the airport wasn't the victory lap I had expected; instead, it was a quiet contemplation of the things I'd heard her say: "I was a good teacher, but that doesn't mean I know how to be a leader." This statement kept ringing through my head over and over. By all accounts, this young woman was not a *good* teacher; she was an *incredible* teacher. She had been recognized locally and nationally for her instructional prowess, all while working incredibly hard to pursue her continued education and certification. This was a rockstar educator who any school would have been thrilled to have as a leader.

However, despite all she had done for students or the things she professionally accomplished on her own, she was buckling under the weight of leadership. She saw me as an expert, but if she had never been willing to be vulnerable herself, she would have never known just how much we had in common. It was that evening, on the flight home, when I made the decision to write this book. This phenomenal young educator was not unlike me and perhaps not unlike you; however, only her willingness to take that risk gave me the chance to understand and bring value to her experience.

The Journey to Wellness

My pathway to this book has been anything but traditional. Over the next few chapters, you'll have a front-row seat to the bumps and bruises that helped me see myself and my colleagues through a completely different lens. You'll find research and information about best practices, but you'll also find a great many lessons learned from the school of hard knocks. The reason for this approach is simple but intentional. In my experience working with leaders throughout the United States, I've found that educators and leaders tend to be pretty good at "faking it." Like the young leader who broke down and cried as I stood in her office, many of us are well-polished, professionally pedigreed, and well-spoken—yet quietly, privately crumbling under the weight of our roles.

This book is intended to meet you right where you are, not where you are supposed to be. If you have been placed in leadership, it is fair to assume a few things about you. First, you have shown instructional and professional practice worthy of being elevated to a place of leadership. Second, much of your professional training and mentorship was focused on the job you excelled at before the one you're in now. Sure, we all had to get certain degrees and certifications, but much like a new teacher in the classroom, the value of these academic pursuits begins failing us as soon as the "real life" of our new position sets in. Third, regardless of the role you're in, most of us feel that there are simply too many eyes on us to falter. When things get difficult or when you begin to feel ill-equipped, don't be surprised to hear something along the lines of, "That's why you make the big bucks, boss." If you're anything like me, this only serves to amplify the feelings of self-doubt or imposter syndrome that many leaders privately wrestle with.

Finally, we as leaders are not known for our professional vulnerability. The need to "have it all together" is somehow so baked into our unspoken professional norms that many of us feel as if the challenges of the job reflect our personal inadequacies, rather than being universal elements we could learn to improve together.

Thankfully, you can be a great leader without having to sacrifice yourself as a person. In fact, this book will take you through five specific, important, fundamental truths.

1. You are a person with a job in educational leadership; being a principal, superintendent, or instructional leader for your campus or district should not cost you the ability to maintain a healthy, balanced life.

2. Despite the feeling that many of us internalize the idea that only a heroic performance in our role is acceptable, we are human beings. Trust me, you can pretend that you don't require the basic things that all of us need to be healthy, but it won't last long.

3. You can determine the type of leader you become. So many of us live our professional lives reacting to the unyielding challenges of our role rather than defining who we want to be and purposefully and intentionally budgeting our time and resources to prove our leadership identity.

4. Leading people can be messy. Regardless of the success of the system you may be leading, you will inevitably have to lead others through change. All the great training you received as a teacher will provide little help when it comes to guiding people through transformative change. This book will

help you understand those you lead and how to practically and effectively meet their needs like a great teacher with students.

5. You committed to the job of leading a group of educators and students to be their very best—and there's no chance you can do it on your own. Instead of trying to find a way to possibly make yourself "enough," few things are more rewarding than growing leadership in others and watching the organization you lead thrive because of the gifts you've nurtured in others—gifts you simply couldn't bring on your own. In this book, I address this issue, which was one of the most freeing realizations for me as a young leader.

In This Book

Educational leadership is complex and often overwhelming, but it can also be one of the single most rewarding positions in the field of education. In this book, I discuss skills and characteristics that, when prioritized, help leaders be the best version of themselves in both their personal and professional lives. Regardless of your position or the configuration of your school or district, if you lead in education, this book is for you. Each chapter is sequenced intentionally to begin with *you the person* and transition to *you the leader*.

First, being great as a leader should not keep you from being a whole person. Self-doubt and imposter syndrome can create a slippery slope that, when left unchecked, leads to an imbalanced, hurried life. Chapter 1 addresses this head on. To meet the needs of those they lead, educational leaders sometimes make unsustainable effort the proof of their commitment. In this chapter, I discuss balance, the shared qualities of educational leaders that make balance so difficult, the stages through which leaders progress on the path to imbalance, and the practical path to protecting your personal life from your job and restoring balance.

Chapter 2 addresses the basic physical components necessary to be your best as a leader. Unfortunately, physical wellness has become confused with a certain physical image or a pursuit of perfection. This chapter intentionally avoids these misconceptions. Instead of the comparisons and guilt that often accompany ideas of physical wellness, this chapter focuses on the way small changes in how we eat, hydrate, and sleep can make monumental differences in the type of person and leader we are.

The rest of the book helps redefine your work so prioritizing your well-being is sustainable. This begins with intention and purpose. Chapter 3 helps you recognize the type of leader you want to become. It will help you see yourself as a leader, understand what brings you professional joy, and intentionally budget your professional life to maximize time. The information in this chapter is meant to help you recognize what you bring to those you serve. Only then will you be able to amplify others and grow your leadership.

Chapter 4 explores the different facets and challenges of leading change. Over time, almost all leaders find themselves navigating necessary change. Success in this process is very rarely the value of the change or initiative but instead, the ability of the leader to purposefully guide others through the change process. If a leader is grounded in their own well-being and purpose, leading change becomes less overwhelming. This chapter discusses the challenge of leading people through change and provides meaningful approaches to help any leader respectfully guide others to a more promising future for their school or district.

Finally, chapter 5 addresses one of the most essential parts of effective leadership—sharing leadership with others. Leaders should embrace the idea that others can be better than they are in certain areas and use that knowledge to empower those around them. This chapter offers strategies to help you identify the type of people you need on your team and utilize them in an impactful way. Living your professional life trying to be all things to all people not only stretches you to the breaking point but also denies others the opportunity to tap into their unique gifts in supporting their school or district.

The greatest promise of this book is that there are things that, when given your intentional focus, will not only make you a better leader but also preserve you as a human being. You are worthy of the role you have, and you can be great while also being whole. Each chapter of this book provides you with practical ideas and tools to improve your leadership while supporting a healthy, sustainable lifestyle. There are tools and reflection questions that can help you better gauge who you are and how you can find growth and wellness. Ultimately, at the end of this book, it is my hope that you will find strength, direction, and purpose in being your best as a human being and leader. You are worth the effort, and your school deserves to have the best leader you can be.

Balancing Work and Life

From my earliest experiences as a student, I knew music would play a huge part in my life. I loved to play the trumpet, and I couldn't get enough of the feeling of collectively sharing great musical experiences with others. It came as little surprise to anyone who knew me that I would become a band director at the hometown high school where I graduated in Arkansas. Like any young teacher, I wanted to be great. I was the new member of a veteran team, constantly learning and growing. Over time, my skills developed, but it was my work ethic that brought me success.

Unbeknownst to others, my work ethic also helped mask my ever-present anxiety. The band program at my school was traditionally one of the great programs in the state. Every staff member, outside of my brand-new self, was a veteran teacher who had garnered recognition and respect throughout their career. These were not just good teachers; they were the teachers everyone in the state emulated. No one was more aware of this than I was.

While I will forever attribute the successful professional foundation I built as a young teacher to the master educators from whom I learned, it took many years before I recognized how the pressure I felt impacted me as a young man. I was hungry to be successful and wanted to be like them. However, except for the very few of my closest confidantes with whom I shared my true feelings, I felt completely invisible. How could I ever build a name for myself as a young teacher when it made more sense to attribute any success I experienced to the storied professionals I worked with every day? This thought began to consume me. I felt unworthy, unnoticed, and unable to contribute. Without realizing it, I found meaning in a herculean work ethic. No one would ever see me as being as talented as my colleagues, but I would leave no room for doubt when it came to how hard I worked.

I worked all the time, scratching and clawing to outwork my perceived deficiencies. I would get to school an hour and a half before classes started and never get home before 5:00 p.m. I took instruments home every night to improve my technique and studied and listened to music constantly. Working nonstop was producing benefits, though, and I was beginning to believe in myself. However, without realizing it, I taught myself a lesson I would spend the rest of my life trying to unlearn—that the answer to my self-doubt is overwhelming effort.

From the outside, I was an incredible success. I went from a completely unknown newbie to someone who was hard to ignore. My students were succeeding at never-before-seen rates, our bands were exploding with new students, and I had burst on the scene as a band director in my state. Over the course of ten years, my bands received the highest ratings; I put more students in the all-state band than any of my friends; my symphonic band was asked to perform as the state honor band; I was named outstanding young music educator for my state; and I was asked to judge at band competitions throughout my region.

In case you didn't notice it, there was a lot of *I* and *me* in my focus during that time. *I* was getting the recognition *my* hard work warranted. Sure, I loved my students, and I loved seeing them succeed, but I also found the validation I longed for. It was feeding a growing beast inside me that I didn't know existed. Hard work, self-sacrifice, success, recognition, repeat. During these same ten years, very few people knew I missed the first time my son crawled or said his first words. They couldn't see the wife behind the scenes who was trying to be all things to our child while his dad was too focused on his accolades. No one could have known the guilt I shouldered or the pain of a strained marriage. All they saw was what I wanted them to see—success.

This effort, and my success as a teacher, caught the attention of one of my principals, who encouraged me to go back to school so I could become an educational leader. After my certification was completed, I began applying for assistant principal jobs in my district. Early on, I took the news of not being hired as understandable. After all, I was still a very young teacher, and others were likely "in line" ahead of me. That said, when one consolation call turned into two, then three, then four, I began to worry that I may never have the chance to put my new learning and degree to use. For the first time in a while, I was again experiencing the pain of insignificance.

Fresh off my most accomplished year as a band director, I found myself once again donning my lone sports coat for an assistant principal interview in my district. On the way to my interview, I got a call from a friend I had met in graduate school. He asked, "You still want to be an administrator?" There was an opening for an assistant principal in his district. I couldn't help but chuckle a little at the circumstances. I was teaching in the district where I grew up, in the same band room where I fell in love with music. I never even considered leaving my district and, honestly, had no desire to do so.

After the frustration and embarrassment of being overlooked time and again, I started to wonder if I had made a mistake. I had found a method to achieve the recognition I so deeply craved as a band director, but with every failed interview for an administrative job, I felt more and more like the terrified young teacher from a decade ago. Somewhat begrudgingly, I agreed to visit my friend's district to meet the man who was going to be their new junior high principal.

A few days later, I found myself driving to meet this principal, feeling ridiculous. I had just had my fifth interview in my home district in which everyone on the interview panel had a front-row seat to my successes as a young teacher, but still . . . I wasn't what they were looking for. I finally recognized that the missed moments with my son and failures with my wife were the costs of something that had very little to contribute to my next professional goal. Now, I was driving to meet someone I didn't know, in a district I didn't know, about a job in a place I had never been. What made me think I had a chance?

When I arrived, my friend explained there were lots of internal applicants for the job, but he knew I was looking and wanted me to have a chance to meet the new principal, Aaron. Seconds later, Aaron entered the room. Well over six feet tall, with a big barrel chest and a powerful voice, he introduced himself and thrust a gigantic, muscular hand my way for a handshake. He looked the part of the hometown athlete I later learned he was. His stature alone could have been intimidating if not for his huge smile and jovial demeanor.

I quickly realized this was going to be a different experience from my other interviews. Instead, Aaron wanted to know about my family and my interests. I learned we shared mentors, faith, and many friends. Any formality that may have existed at the beginning of our conversation was quickly gone. Instead, it felt as if I was talking to a buddy I hadn't seen in years. We laughed, joked, and made plans to introduce our wives.

On my way out of the office to my car, my brain was swirling. Did we even talk about my professional accolades or the job? I smiled, trying to remember what questions he had asked me. Only when I pulled my cell phone from my jacket pocket did I realize I had been there for nearly two hours.

Over the next three weeks, I made the decision to leave my home district, take a pay cut, and commit to commuting to and from work for one reason only: I wanted to work for Aaron. I couldn't quite articulate why, but he made me want to be my best. He was motivating, encouraging, and humble. I didn't know it at the time, but Aaron would become my best friend. Our families immediately clicked, and my son learned to love his children. In Aaron, I saw the type of leader, person, husband, and father I aspired to become. Aaron, a brand-new principal, and me, his green assistant, learned everything together as we navigated the unknown.

I had the job I wanted with a boss who was like my big brother. However, this didn't keep the self-doubt from creeping back in. The hundreds of hours I spent studying music and practicing instruments offered little value to me now as an assistant principal. No one cared about my bands, and very few understood the world I had left. I was new all over again—unrecognized, intimidated, and unworthy. So, I did what I had learned would help me succeed: I got to work first every day and was the last to leave. I wanted everyone in the school to see that what I lacked in experience, I would make up in time and hard work.

One day, early in the year, Aaron came to my office, closed the door, and told me we needed to talk. His typically jovial, carefree nature was gone, and a blank, serious stare was in its place. Nervously, I wracked my brain for the things I could have messed up, but before I could ask, he looked me in the eye and said, "This job isn't worth what you're spending on it."

Puzzled, I started to ask him what he meant before he cut me off, "Josh, why are you spending so much time away from your family? You're just up here working by yourself. I'm not going to allow you to do that."

My first reaction was defensive. I wanted to tell him that I had everything under control—I was a hard worker, and this was the person he hired. Instead, the truth began to spill out of my mouth as my eyes stung with tears, threatening to make me look weak in front of my new hero. With a wavering voice, I explained how as a band director, I had missed many family milestones and strained my relationship with my wife—all for a job that I left.

I felt so selfish—I had exposed the true version of myself to someone I wanted so badly to impress. But where I expected judgment from him, instead, I got understanding. He shared how his family paid dearly for his professional decisions, too. When he realized this, he did the only thing he felt he could—he left the job that was threatening what he loved. He only came back to leadership when he and his family had a plan for how it would not cost them so dearly. He ended with a statement I had never once heard from a leader: "When I hired you for this job, I hired you as a man, a husband, and a dad. Nothing about this job is worth damaging what matters most to us."

Your story is undoubtedly different than mine. What unites us is the unyielding pressure of leading in education. Being great at your job shouldn't diminish your life. While you may or may not have outside influences that push you toward imbalance, it is so easy for all of us to push ourselves that way. Understanding ourselves, recognizing how pressure can influence us, and refusing to sacrifice what matters most not only protects us as people; it also makes us better for those we lead.

About Balance

Aaron changed my life as a young leader, but I wish I could tell you he helped me solve my problem with imbalance. Personally, my recurring struggle with balance started as a young teacher and has been my unintended go-to at different points in my leadership journey. Later in this chapter, I will explore the path many take on their way to imbalance; but first, let's take a moment to better understand what balance means.

A balanced life likely means something a little different for each of us. As I consider my life, balance was much different as a single man than it is as a husband and father of two active children. For the purposes of this book, I would define *balance* as a leader's ability to thrive both professionally and personally. Balance is more a pursuit than a destination. Each of us has professional and personal goals that drive us toward a future we envision, but balance exists in the present. In our busy lives, sometimes our ability to determine our balance, like our physical wellness, comes down to the symptoms we are experiencing.

If balance is a state in which we can thrive, *imbalance* is a state in which we struggle to survive. According to Al James (2014), the most cited symptoms of professional and personal imbalance are "missing out on children's activities, interrupted sleep patterns, stress and exhaustion impacting relationships, working when feeling unwell, missing out on leisure time and hobbies, and an overall reduced quality of life" (p. 289). In case you're feeling a little exposed right now, my buddy Aaron would say, "Come on in; the water's fine." In other words, you're in good company, friend.

For me, imbalance brought anxiety, isolation, and stress. Over time, I became accustomed to working this way and never stopped to consider how these powerful emotions drastically changed my behavior. My year working with Aaron was like an oasis because I had a leader who expected and reinforced good balance in my life. However, this was a short-lived time in my life, as I would take on my first principalship a year later. As my career progressed, I no longer had a boss who could help keep me in check. Instead, like in my early teaching years, what Aaron helped me prioritize, I chose to ignore.

However, my wife saw the things I chose to overlook. The imbalance of my band-directing years was behind me, but I was losing the fight on new fronts as a leader. My phone controlled me. I felt the need to be constantly "on call," so I could, at any moment, be ready to meet the needs of those I led. My evenings were spent discussing and planning for the next day, which meant I was communicating with colleagues and staff outside of work hours and establishing a professional norm of being "on call" for those I led as well.

I wasn't missing out on as many important family milestones as before, but while I was "there," I was often distracted by my choice to constantly juggle my personal and professional lives. The pressure I felt to be visible at every nighttime event at school meant I was physically fatigued, regularly fighting sickness, and as you can probably imagine, not very fun to live with.

Even though I had personally felt the pain of this type of lifestyle before, it took the hurt in my wife's eyes for me to recognize how imbalance was changing me. Without an Aaron to keep me in check or a courageously honest wife unwilling to live the life she had experienced before, I may have never recognized how much I was controlled by my fear of failure.

Fear of failure has a powerful hold on many leaders like me. These fears and emotions, and the behaviors they cause, form a cycle that is incredibly hard to break. A professional norm of always being on call means that others expect round-the-clock availability. Leaders who establish themselves as the constant problem solver can inadvertently train others to develop further dependency on them. Over time, a lack of attention to boundaries can become the professional expectations others hold us to.

It's not at all hard to imagine how these things can consume leaders. The needs increase, while the hours don't. Ultimately, something must give. Many times, while leaders convince themselves they can keep going, their bodies say otherwise. This is part of the reason imbalance is so strongly correlated with absenteeism (Ngwenya & Utete, 2023). The more imbalanced we are, the more likely we are to have both planned and unplanned absences from work, even though most educational leaders would tell you that few things are harder than recovering after missing a day of work.

Thankfully, leaders can avoid finding themselves in this place! If you find yourself feeling overwhelmed by imbalance, there are practical steps to find peace and balance. This begins with knowing ourselves as educational leaders. By understanding what most leaders share in common, there is a pathway to finding balance for us and our entire profession.

Who Becomes an Educational Leader

While they may have had other leadership opportunities beyond the traditional school leadership roles, most educational leaders started their journey in the classroom (Liebowitz & Porter, 2020). Before that, they chose to become teachers. As educators, we knew we would never reach great social status or wealth, but the thought of helping students, of making a difference in their lives, was so enticing we decided to make it our life's pursuit. This largely singular pathway from classroom teacher to leader is unique when compared to leaders in other professional fields. Imagine if all corporate CEOs began only as accountants or entrepreneurs. Instead, in the professional world, leaders come from many different professional backgrounds. For those of us in educational leadership, our origin stories are much less diverse. Our common experiences give us the unique opportunity to understand and support one another.

This realization first occurred to me on the heels of what could only be described as a physical breakdown, which I'll share more about in the next chapter. As I worked through my own physical issues, I began hearing stories of other leaders that sounded eerily like mine. At the time, I was a doctoral student at the University of Arkansas. As I shared my story, I learned from colleagues how common these types of struggles were. I wanted to know what was behind this struggle. Was it the job? Was it the person? How could we find a way to help support one another so no one had to hit rock bottom the way so many leaders seemed to do?

These questions became the basis for unprecedented research in my home state of Arkansas. Years before I assumed my first leadership position, Gary Hopkins (2009) described my experience perfectly when he said:

> When they entered the profession, most principals and assistant principals knew their lives were about to change. . . . They didn't realize that if they were not careful or organized or able to say "no," the work hours might consume them. If the guilt of missing family events to tend to school business didn't eat them alive first, that is.

With the stark reality of these words fresh in my mind, I set out to learn how widespread this experience was.

More than five hundred leaders participated in a survey aimed at understanding their personal state of balance (Hopkins, 2009). It asked about their basic physiological well-being, including sleep, hydration, and nutrition. It asked leaders to share their workload, the amount of time they spent working from home, and their ability to enjoy hobbies and leisure activities outside of work. The survey results were both sobering and powerful. However, I couldn't help feeling these survey results only told part of the story. I needed to hear directly from leaders—those who were struggling to achieve balance as well as those who had found a way to set boundaries around the things that mattered most. To do this, I used the survey results to create two different groups of leaders—those who expressed balance as nearly impossible and those who had found a way to protect what mattered most while doing their job.

As I analyzed the results in 2019, I recognized my own experience, and the one Hopkins (2009) described fifteen years ago, and how both echoed the responses of my colleagues. Like me, time with their loved ones mattered most to them. Unfortunately, also like me, what mattered most often lost out to the pressures of their role. Leaders across Arkansas were enjoying less than two hours a day with the most important people in their lives and nearly a third of them couldn't even manage to find an hour to spend with their loved ones (Ray, 2019). Over half the leaders admitted having to choose work over loved ones at least three times each week (Ray, 2019). Was this a conscious choice? Did someone or something make them do this, or had they done it to themselves?

The Stages of Leadership Imbalance

In no time at all, it became clear that I wanted more than simply to know the current state of leaders. I had to know what was behind the imbalance threatening so many of my colleagues. I needed to hear from practicing leaders and allow them to share their own stories. Armed with the survey results and a clear picture of the widespread imbalance leaders experienced, I formed two groups to hear the stories behind their experiences. Unbeknownst to the leaders, I had grouped them intentionally based on what their answers to the survey said about their lifestyle. One group found themselves at the mercy of their job. Caring for themselves or those they loved was undoubtedly a priority, but one that was in direct competition with what they felt the job required. The second group was distinctly different from the first. Either through self-prioritization or recognition of the toll the job was taking, this group found a way to protect what mattered most while succeeding in their role.

Over the course of several weeks, I had the chance to hear from the first group of leaders whose survey responses suggested they were struggling to find balance. It became clear how a real and relatable fear seemed to lurk behind every subconscious choice to deny what mattered most to them, as it did for me.

While each story was unique, there was a three-stage progression in which relatable fear seemed to take control. This fear stemmed from their own insecurities. They were afraid to fail and to hurt those they led. Over time, this fear would progress to stage one—imposter syndrome. During this stage, leaders feel inadequate, worry about their ability to meet the needs of those they lead, and look for ways to find areas of confidence.

Like me, these leaders took a singular approach to their feelings of professional inadequacy—stage two—unbridled, unsustainable effort. This effort, beyond what anyone would reasonably expect, brought them recognition and a measure of success. They began to be known for this effort and referenced the many times those they led affirmed their work ethic. Naturally, this made them proud and provided a salve to the pain of imposter syndrome. However, as people around them began to expect this effort, the leaders gave more and more to continue receiving the recognition they craved.

Ultimately, they felt they had no choice but to resort to the last of the three stages of leadership imbalance—self-sacrifice—all for the sake of the recognized effort they practiced. At this final stage, the cost of time and effort required to continue receiving the affirmation the leaders craved came at the cost of things that mattered deeply to them. They or those closest to them were beginning to recognize that their pathway to success would come at a high personal cost.

Each of these leaders was seemingly ensnared by a trap of their own design. They had inadvertently trained others to expect the unsustainable effort that they chose to overcome their own self-doubt. While each was resolute in understanding what mattered most, they found themselves with an impossible decision. Did they choose to pull back on the unsustainable effort that helped them feel successful, or did they sacrifice whatever was necessary to avoid the failure that so terrified them? Ultimately, they found ways to ease the weight of the second option. They convinced themselves this effort was just what the job requires or even that it would get easier one day. The problem was that "one day" never came. By the time I met them, they were exhausted, emotionally bankrupt, and feeling hopeless. To protect ourselves from the slippery slope of these stages to burnout, we must understand them and recognize them.

Stage 1: Imposter Syndrome

What is *imposter syndrome*? You might be familiar with this term. According to *Psychology Today* (n.d.), imposter syndrome occurs when people "believe that they are undeserving of their achievements and the high esteem in which they are, in fact, generally held." This syndrome is common in many leaders and can lead to fear and anxiety.

I remember when I completed my degree to be an administrator. After two years of graduate classes, summers spent in college classrooms instead of with my new wife, and more papers than I could have imagined writing, the list of observation hours I was supposed to log at the end of my educational leadership degree was daunting to the point of almost seeming silly. I took the list of required hours to my mentor administrator and painstakingly explained the many requirements I was supposed to complete. A smirk crept across his face, and he raised his hand to stop me mid-sentence. "Just bring it to me when you need me to sign it," he said.

We did our best to create some meaningful learning opportunities for me. I would occasionally sit in with him to discuss things he was doing. I helped order food for our embedded professional development day, and he included me in some emails. And three months later, I graduated and was fully certified as a building administrator. I wasn't sure at the time when or if I would become a leader; I really wasn't too concerned with how little I knew about the job for which I was now certified.

However, just a few years later as a new assistant principal, it quickly became clear how little I knew about my new job. All the time and effort I'd spent over the last ten years learning to teach students to play musical instruments offered little value when it came time to plan an active shooter drill, call an upset parent, or plan professional learning, much less evaluate teachers in content areas I knew nothing about.

Like me, the imbalanced leaders I studied were intimately aware of the things they didn't know. They were teachers and coaches—great at interacting with students and instructing—but also like me, never felt equipped to perform the tasks of the administrative role they held. It wasn't until they assumed their new role that they began to understand how much they needed to learn—and quickly.

In his book *Schoolteacher*, Dan C. Lortie (1975) calls education "an apprenticeship of observation" (p. 67), in which teachers and leaders consider most professional learning to occur on the job. Lortie knew in 1975 what leaders and teachers feel today; degrees and certifications are important, but we learn on the job. Being new and green as a teacher is daunting. However, in the stories of these leaders, I heard the concern I felt. What were those we led supposed to do while we were "figuring it all out" on the job? Who wants a leader who doesn't know the answers? And let us not forget the words of the educator I described in the introduction to this book: "I was a good teacher, but that doesn't mean I know how to be a leader."

Many leaders wrestling with this anxiety did precisely what I planned to do as a new leader. Unsure they could be all the things their school needed, they hoped they could overcome their lack of knowledge with service and effort. It was clear the change from a respected teacher or coach to a seemingly ignorant leader was hard on these leaders. For them, fear of exposure, disappointment, and failure drove many of them to revert to the very thing Aaron refused to allow me to do as his assistant: try to outwork their insecurities.

Stage 2: Unsustainable Effort

"I may not know how to help teachers with teaching reading, but I can come in early and stay late to keep things off their plate." The words had barely left the mouth of one new leader in my study before the rest of the imbalanced leaders I was studying provided near-immediate affirmation. As a researcher, my job was to record what I heard, note the body language, try to count the nodding heads, and capture the person who responded with "exactly." However, as a person who had personally experienced the danger of this statement, everything within me wanted to cry out.

As I watched, it was clear by the others' responses that there was more than simply an agreement with the things this leader expressed. In fact, it felt more like a respectful appreciation among a group of people who understood one another. These weren't just answers to questions; we were hitting at the fundamental elements of their experiences as leaders. They weren't simply agreeing with each other; they were validating each other's decision to try to overcompensate for their often-skewed self-perceptions.

To the average person, these imbalanced leaders were impressive people. They ranged from one first-year leader all the way to someone in their twenty-third year in educational leadership, and each clearly cared deeply about their school. They might have called themselves servant leaders. Robert K. Greenleaf introduced the term *servant leadership* in 1970 (Greenleaf Center for Servant Leadership, n.d.). Greenleaf explains that servant leaders are unique because they are servants first instead of leaders first.

Greenleaf also explains that the difference between servant leaders and other leaders typically shows up in the "care taken by the servant-first to make sure that other people's highest priority needs are being served" (as cited in Greenleaf Center for Servant Leadership, n.d.). These leaders matched Greenleaf's depiction by prioritizing taking care of those they led.

As we talked together, what initially felt like a rigid, formal conversation soon melted into a comfort resembling a reunion. Privately, I would look forward to meeting with these leaders for several days before our appointments. In hindsight, I realize now how affirming their conversation was, but it was more than that. This was a group of people you simply couldn't help but enjoy being around—funny, kind, and genuine. I found myself feeling almost intimidated by the passion with which they spoke about their schools and those they served. Over time, these emotions I worked hard to check as a researcher became conflicting. I realized the nature of their personalities, the constant service-minded approach they brought to work daily, was somehow entangled with the reality that they were living lives that were desperately imbalanced.

I am not suggesting that leaders serving others or putting forth great effort is negative in any way. However, as was the case with these leaders, effort as an answer to lack of skill or knowledge can present a type of "blank check" approach to those we lead. If our value is found in our ability to constantly do more and more, then setting limits to preserve balance in our lives threatens what makes us valuable in the eyes of those we lead. Over time, as the repeated answer to keep from "letting others down" becomes more and more effort on the part of the leader, something must give. Unfortunately, for the leaders I studied, the "something that gave" was almost always them.

Stage 3: Self-Sacrifice

The growing internal conflict I felt between my desire to try to emulate these leaders and their self-reported unsustainable lives was coming to a head. I could completely relate, as they vulnerably expressed their own versions of fear of failure. I also knew firsthand what it was like to try to outwork my own professional insecurities. What was I missing?

Then, it hit me like a lightning bolt. Like many times before, I was recording the conversation and noting collective affirmation from those in the room when it became clear to me these leaders weren't choosing to sacrifice for those they led; they had become defined by this sacrifice. As leader after leader shared their stories, I noticed the emotions behind the affirmations coming from their peers. Self-sacrifice and the "cost of the job" became the common ground on which they found validation from one another. There was an unspoken belief that while each of them felt as if they were personally crumbling, what they were doing was right or necessary to be a good leader.

I realized their perceived self-value was directly tied to the affirmation they received from others for their unsustainable selflessness. Self-sacrifice had become an expectation that was controlling them. When faced with the impossibility of taking care of themselves or continuing to take care of others, they were willing to deny themselves because choosing anything else might compromise their professional "success."

"You want to take care of everybody else. You want to take care of the students at your school. What little time you have left, you think, 'I can't use this time on me,'" one leader shared. Another agreed, "I honestly think that it's our need to help everybody else, students first . . . and we're willing to back off on our own health and well-being to make sure those students get what they need to be successful." While these sentiments are noble, they are completely unsustainable and represent the pathway many leaders take.

Leaders do not plan to deny themselves or those they love. We need to have a powerful motivator to drive us to accept an unbalanced life. In this group of leaders, and even for me, the motivator was simple: fear. Fear of failure drives leaders to do whatever it takes to find success, even if what it takes is completely unsustainable. In fact, for many of us, it is only when we can stop and take a moment to appreciate the power this fear holds over us that we begin to see just how unsustainable the pace of our lives has become.

I wish I could have written this chapter in time for those leaders. I heard them collectively share the same path I had experienced. I felt their isolation and the feelings of helplessness they shared amid the all-consuming schedule they fought so hard to sustain. They were charming, caring people with whom I could have easily seen building friendships. They were great teachers who dedicated their lives to the students they served, but it was obvious they were so out of balance that they were hurtling down an unsustainable path.

At the time, I felt helpless. I was a researcher tasked with documenting their experiences while quietly wrestling with the same self-imposed pressures they endured. I wish I could go back, turn off the recorder, and implore them to see that this is not the only way to be successful. Today, not one of the leaders I spoke to is still in the same role. Even more tragically, four of them have since passed away.

Imbalance Versus Balance

Finding our way out of an imbalanced life, or even living in purposeful balance, begins with an understanding of the motivations behind each of these states. It would be simple enough to make a list of things we might do if we want to maintain a greater margin in our lives. However, choosing to ignore the emotions and psychology behind imbalance would be akin to offering a heart patient a Band-Aid. Imbalance is a symptom. Therefore, to heal any imbalance in our life, we must first diagnose the root of the issue. Only then will we experience meaningful, lasting change.

Sources of Imbalance

If you realize you could be on the path to self-sacrifice, my hope is that the rest of this chapter might be your life preserver. That said, the practical tips and ideas to come will stand little chance if pitted against the emotions or fears that start each of us down the descent to imbalance. I hope to do more than simply save you from your current imbalance. Instead, when you understand how you became imbalanced and what beliefs controlled your behaviors, you have a better chance of never struggling to keep your head above water again. Specifically, I am referring to the fears that start one on the path to imposter syndrome. Like so much of this book, these fears are unique to you and the school or district in which you serve. However, in every situation where leaders find themselves committed to more than they could ever maintain, it likely began with simple, relatable fear.

For me, fear took on different forms in every new role I encountered. As a band director, I was afraid of being exposed as a rookie teacher. I was worried the team of veteran teachers who hired me might regret the decision if I couldn't manage to be more than they expected. As an elementary principal, my lack of content knowledge caused me to fear being incapable of being an instructional leader. After all, my experience was as a high school band director!

The first time I heard an elementary mathematics teacher say the word *subitize*, I wasn't even sure I could spell it, much less understand what they were talking about. How could I possibly lead these teachers to get better? Even now, as someone who travels the country to work with other schools, I still find myself afraid that I won't be enough to meet the needs of teachers in a community and school where I have never worked. Professional fear is natural and real; it is a symptom of leadership, and dealing with it in one position does not mean it won't sprout back up as something completely different down the line.

The danger with these fears is that they grow. They morph and change into lies we tell ourselves so regularly that it becomes difficult to separate reality from the false narrative fear creates for us. This happens when fears become assumptions that drive our behaviors. For example, as a young elementary principal, my fear of being exposed as someone ignorant of the content our teachers were discussing became an assumption that had power over my behaviors. If teachers knew I didn't know what they were talking about, I assumed I would surely lose all credibility as a leader. The teachers would start to wonder why our district even hired me in the first place (which, by the way, I was starting to wonder myself).

When teachers realized this, surely, they would talk to each other about it. Our small community would think they made a mistake choosing me for elementary principal, and soon, I would be ousted from the job—I'd be the failure I felt like every single time I encountered another thing I didn't understand. Rejected and embarrassed, I would have to pull my son from the school and move to a different town.

While this seems silly even now as I write it, most people will admit they've been down this same path in their mind. Maybe we try to convince ourselves it's ridiculous, but deep down, fear keeps gaining strength. In my case, guess who I was fooling? Not a single person. Every teacher in that room knew I had never worked in an elementary school. However, because of my building fear, I was staying late to read about curriculum, calling people I trusted to catch me up in the evenings, and devoting a monumental amount of time outside my job attempting to fake others into thinking I was something other than who I really was.

I let fear, a very rational fear, turn into imposter syndrome and push me to do whatever it took to not embarrass myself or fail our school. I wish I could go back in time and tell myself, "Hey dummy, everyone knows you were a high school band director. What makes you think they would expect you to be an expert in kindergarten instruction in your first year? Why don't you be honest, admit the areas that everyone already knows you will be learning, celebrate the greatness of the instructional leaders currently in the building, and focus on doing your best?" It seems so simple with the clarity of hindsight.

If you are experiencing fear as a leader, chances are it is very rational and understandable. However, know that if you leave it unaddressed, it will morph, change, and metastasize into something that could completely change your behaviors professionally and personally. I encourage you to work through the fear-to-behavior tool in figure 1.1. It is meant to help you regain some of the control our professional fears rob from us. It will help you name a fear, consider the assumptions it is causing, and identify your behaviors because of these assumptions. When we can pull the fears and assumptions into the light, they are rarely as powerful as they are in the quiet of our own insecurities.

Fear I Am Experiencing as a Leader	Assumptions Tied to This Fear	Behaviors Driven by This Assumption	What I Could Do Differently
Example: Fear of content knowledge exposure	Example: Loss of credibility; being seen as a weak leader; those I lead will question my placement; I may fail in this role	Example: Staying late to study curriculum; calling people every night to ask questions; staying up late to watch teaching videos; skipping my son's T-ball game the night before a team meeting; spending large periods of the weekend learning curricula	Example: Admit what I don't know; learn with the teachers instead of in private; learn from other instructional leaders in the building; celebrate the strengths of others in this area

Figure 1.1: Fear-to-behavior tool.

*Visit **go.SolutionTree.com/educatorwellness** for a blank reproducible version of this figure.*

Elements of Balance

There is a sobriety that only comes when we acknowledge the grip these fears have on our actions. However, as I shared earlier, my reverence for Aaron's direction and even my love for my family were not enough to completely save me from the draw of imbalance. I had to realize the lie behind imbalance—the idea that more and more is the same as better and better.

In his book *The Happiness Advantage*, Shawn Achor (2010) attacks the fundamental belief that I brought to work every day. Achor (2010) writes that many people believe professional happiness or fulfillment is the result of success. Instead, he suggests that happiness, or positive psychology, should be seen as a precursor to success rather than the goal one aspires to. His point is backed by research on the power of positive psychology. For example, Barbara L. Fredrickson's (2001) broaden-and-build theory suggests that positive emotions broaden our ability to think and act in different ways, resulting in stronger social connections, coping skills, and resilience. Also, there is a strong correlation between our positive emotions and our performance in some of the most key functions of being a leader—creativity, productivity, and decision making (Lyubomirsky, King, & Diener, 2005).

At the beginning of this chapter, I defined balance as our ability to thrive instead of merely survive in our professional and personal lives. Survival, the symptom of imbalance, robs us of our positive emotions and, in turn, threatens our happiness as well as our effectiveness. Survival is not something leaders must endure to hold onto success. In fact, imbalance compromises our ability to perform some of the most fundamental components of educational leadership well.

Achor (2010) suggests happiness is an action that requires intentionality. Similarly, balance requires us to be intentional and purposeful to keep from sliding into a crushing, unsustainable place. Imbalance is painful, unsustainable, and scary. Thankfully, it is also completely unnecessary. With intention and purpose, leaders can be well while also being their best professionally and personally.

Finding balance is not impossible, but it doesn't happen by accident. Those who lead while maintaining balance recognize when their balance is being threatened. Often, those closest to them may bring this to their attention first. The recognition of imbalance is only corrected when we become self-aware. By considering how we got to a place of imbalance and understanding even the subconscious motivators behind our behaviors, we can then begin to make small changes. However, these changes in private are vulnerable. Until we communicate and practice adjusted limits, we are much more likely to fall unceremoniously back into our state of hurry and imbalance.

Intentional Balance

While I learned a lot from my time spent with the twenty leaders who struggled to find balance, another group was equally impactful. This group had clearly found a way to create the margin in their lives that others struggled with. At first, having personally struggled so much with my own imbalance, I wanted to believe that somehow balance was easier for them. Maybe there was some personality type or character trait that made someone more likely to live a balanced life. Admittedly, this skewed reality would have been a little easier on my ego than the truth. One by one, these leaders shared a conscious decision they made to make balance a priority. Balance wasn't a character trait or a happy accident. It was an *intentional goal* toward which they consciously and intentionally strived.

This was a watershed moment for me as a researcher and leader. Balanced leaders weren't different or better than imbalanced leaders. In fact, they experienced many of the same things as the leaders who were hurtling headfirst toward burnout. The only difference for these balanced leaders was the recognition and decision to place intentional boundaries in their lives. There are no balanced and imbalanced people; the only difference is the intentionality some leaders place on finding balance in their lives.

If you want to live a balanced life, it takes *intentional effort*. For each of us, this means something different. When we find ourselves in a state of imbalance, we can become so focused on our areas of weakness and our perceived inability to improve that we can unintentionally give these weaknesses even more power over us. Improvement is incremental, and many of us find clarity and the path to a better life in strength in our most precious relationships.

Among these balanced leaders, there were clear patterns. Like their peers who were struggling, many of these leaders described a time when they were out of balance. Then, one by one, each mentioned a particular person in their life that helped them recognize the destructive potential of their chosen lifestyle. As you read this, you may know exactly who this person is in your life. Maybe you have heard from those who love you most that your pace seems to be taking a toll.

In contrast to the deficiency mindset that might suggest balanced leaders were always balanced, the opposite was true. Instead, with the help of those most committed to their personal well-being, they found a pathway to a new reality through self-awareness, communicated limits, and accountability.

Recognition

One of my greatest struggles with imbalance was my unwillingness to admit I was trying to juggle too much. This wasn't the case for every leader I met with. Some knew their limits before entering the job. However, most heard it first from a spouse, a best friend, or someone close in their life. Amid imbalance, leaders work hard to maintain the pace that has provided them with some measure of success. This focus makes it easy to not notice the building symptoms of fatigue or burnout that start to emerge.

However, for those who know us best, changes we might overlook are much more obvious. If, in reading this chapter, you recognize your own state of imbalance, it is highly likely that someone else recognized it first. When we believe that imbalance is just a reality educational leaders must accept, the concerns of our loved ones are more easily dismissed. However, as you read this chapter and recognize that success doesn't have to come at the cost of what matters most, concerns from those closest to you might take on a different light. While balance is a worthy pursuit, when you are your best, your school will get the best version of you as a leader. In other words, the concerns of those who care most about you may influence not only who you are as a person but also your ability to be your best as a leader.

Regardless of how we recognize that our professional and personal balance are unsustainable, until this happens, we will go on pretending we can continue the breakneck pace we are struggling to maintain. With this recognition, though, we can ask what we are willing to give and what we need from our profession to maintain a healthy relationship with our work. This approach allows us to regain some control over our schedules but also our identity. No longer do we have to "do what it takes" to uphold our professional identity. Instead, we can approach our jobs by recognizing who we are and what we need to be while serving as leaders. Different than the first group of leaders, who expressed helplessness in unsustainable effort, this purposeful approach provides boundaries that can protect us. It also helps protect us from resentment that can occur when we feel our lives are controlled by our job (Esposito, 2019).

Self-Awareness

Successful change is incremental. Someone who wants to run a marathon can't run twenty miles their first time out. Similarly, leaders don't immediately find themselves in a state of imbalance. It takes time and patience to regain a healthy balance, but that is OK! We can't change everything in our professional lives all at once, but we can start making small changes that have impact. If others have learned to depend on you, simply explaining that you need to focus on balance may not be enough. That said, something as simple as plugging in your phone in a different room at night could provide you enough mental rest to be fully present with your loved ones.

The balanced leaders in my study clearly understood the priorities in their lives. This didn't occur overnight, but by taking things slow and making small adjustments in areas that matter most, they built life-changing habits over time (Esposito, 2019). One leader in my study explained that his struggle to disconnect from work was causing strain on his marriage. Together with his wife, he established a nightly routine of "no-tech talk" when they just sat and reconnected at the end of each busy day. Another leader explained that coaching her girls' little league teams was something she was unwilling to give up. She adjusted her evening school supervision schedule to ensure she was able to do this. One by one, they each expressed recognition and chose to define what was sacred to them and protect it at all costs.

Communicated Limits

It was clear that balance was important not just for these leaders but also for those they led. As we talked, I learned how they brought a newfound approach to their leadership and communicated it clearly with colleagues. There were very specific boundary-building behaviors these leaders embodied. They established their limits, became comfortable with saying no, were direct, didn't allow fear or guilt to derail the goals they set for themselves, and were role models for those they led.

What started as a leader's individual commitment gave license to others to prioritize balance for themselves. The leader who enjoyed uninterrupted conversation with his spouse each evening explained to his staff that he was setting a poor example by emailing outside of hours. He only realized this when he committed to disconnecting and protecting a section of each evening. With this recognition, he promised his staff he would limit the amount of communication he sent outside of work hours with the kind request that they follow suit. His vulnerability changed the culture of the school and promoted better balance for everyone.

These stories were incredibly uplifting for me. Instead of finding disappointment among those they led, these leaders' vulnerability was uniting and empowering. They may not have anticipated that they were not the only ones in their school who were stretched thin. Leading by example allowed others the opportunity to see that they too could be effective, successful, *and* whole.

Consider your school or district. Can you think of people who might benefit from a leader who led in such a way? If we follow the example of leading with vulnerability in our pursuit of balance, we can make those we lead feel worthy of a similar pursuit.

Accountability

When we identify the changes we want to make and communicate them with clarity and vulnerability, we can hold ourselves and one another accountable. Like the leader who stopped evening work communication, leaders can build a culture of healthy balance for everyone they serve. My mentor, Aaron, would have likely professionally benefitted from having an assistant principal like me—so driven to prove myself that I was willing to work all hours of the day to be successful. However, Aaron cared enough about me that he was willing to help me change for the better.

You have people in your life who care enough to value your ability to thrive both personally and professionally. These are the same people who might recognize the symptoms of imbalance in your life before you do. Accountability is as easy as asking these people to simply check in on the small choices you have committed to. Not a single leader I studied *wanted* to live a life out of balance. They wanted to be great educational leaders so much that some didn't recognize how little their compromised self could offer those they led. That is why we need people, in either our personal or professional lives, who are willing to respectfully remind us of what matters most to us.

Now, stop and reflect on the level of balance in your personal and professional life (see page 26). Record your thoughts in a notebook or journal.

Stop and Reflect: What Is Your Current Level of Balance?

Take a moment to think about your current level of balance. Are you spreading yourself too thin? Do you take the time to do things you enjoy? What do your friends and family say about your balance (or lack thereof)? Are you honest with yourself and others about your needs, and do you take steps to get those needs met?

Record your thoughts before you continue reading.

Strategies to Help You Find Balance

This section describes three simple strategies you can use to find balance in your personal and professional life: (1) use a self-awareness tool, (2) identify and protect what matters most, and (3) practice caring accountability.

Use a Self-Awareness Tool

What is your current level of balance? Do you allow your personal and professional lives to thrive? To help you with these questions, see figure 1.2.

Personal

In my personal life, I am happiest when I:

In my personal life, I have the greatest impact when I:

How many times each week do I fully engage in this?

What is in the way of me fully engaging in this?

Professional

In my professional life, I am happiest when I:

In my professional life, I have the greatest impact when I:

How many times each week do I fully engage in this?

What is in the way of me fully engaging in this?

Figure 1.2: Personal and professional priorities tool.

*Visit **go.SolutionTree.com/educatorwellness** for a free reproducible version of this figure.*

Perhaps this chapter will help you realize a need for more balance in your life. With the understanding that you can't fix everything at once, it's important to prioritize a few things worth the time and effort to adjust. What matters most to you personally and professionally, and what role do these things have in your life? From there, you can use this tool to consider what could be standing in the way of your ability to get more of "the good stuff" in your personal and professional life.

This tool could also provide valuable feedback from those who care deeply about you. They will have an outsider's perspective where you are most fulfilled. They may also see areas of stress or conflict that could unnecessarily keep you from the very things that matter most to you. Sharing this with a loved one provides perspective and accountability that could be hard to accomplish on your own.

Personally, I have learned the importance of being with my family. When I can protect my time with them, I feel like my internal battery is recharged to face whatever the next day has in store. I have also learned that I love working side by side with teachers and leaders. Sure, my job requires many things of me throughout the day, but I made the decision to spend time in team meetings and with principals in my district. I specifically carve time out of my day to leave my office and be with teachers and leaders, regardless of how busy I am.

I have worked hard to be fully present with my family when I am home at night. They bring me so much joy that it is easy to fully enjoy my time with them if I can make myself disconnect. And because fishing is my favorite hobby, I plan fishing trips with my friends and family throughout the year. I space them out, so I have a chance to do something I truly love every few months. These sound like simple things, but collectively, they make joy a priority in my professional and personal life.

Identify and Protect What Matters Most

Throughout this chapter, I've discussed some of the draws that pull us, often unknowingly, toward a life of imbalance. While I can encourage you to see the importance of balance, and even how it can improve key components of your leadership, there will never be a motivator as strong as what matters most to you. As noted previously, one of the falsehoods that lead us to imbalance is the belief that we must continue to overextend ourselves to be successful. Often, we don't recognize all the time engulfed by our professional drive came at a cost somewhere else in our lives until we find ourselves in a moment of pain.

For me, the costs were substantial. Thanks to the strength of an incredible wife and the resiliency of two great boys, my relationship with those I love most is stronger than ever. Still, there are experiences I never had and memories I'll never know because I chose to spend my time focusing on crippling self-doubt instead of turning work off to attend to what mattered most to me. If, instead, I had made a conscious effort to draw lines in the sand to protect my priorities, I may not have experienced the pain of imbalance. If you've never taken a moment to do this, use the tool in figure 1.3 to make an honest appraisal of what you care most about and create a plan to protect it.

What matters most to me in my life?	What about my professional role threatens this the most?	How could I actively protect what matters most from the distractions of this professional role?

Figure 1.3: Priority protection tool.

Visit **go.SolutionTree.com/educatorwellness** *for a free reproducible version of this figure.*

I do not let myself go more than two days without interacting with the principals I work alongside. If I let myself get caught up with the "junk" of my job, I find myself lacking purpose. When I can support my leaders, I feel impactful and purposeful. I have had to set boundaries around my evenings with colleagues to be present with my family. I have also had very intentional conversations with those in my office to help them understand where I am and what I'm doing when I am not sitting at my desk. This may seem simple, but otherwise, I might be worried that people thought I was out of my office too much. I know where I am at my best and have been intentional to make it a priority each day.

Practice Caring Accountability

As leaders, we set an example for those we lead. Communicating your priorities gives license to those around you to find healthy balance themselves. With recognition and the clarity of self-awareness, communicate the changes others may experience when working with you. To the point you are comfortable, be vulnerable and honest.

As you progress through this book, you will experience the ups and downs of my personal story. I made a conscious choice to be this vulnerable. Sure, I could write to you like an "expert," as someone who has it all figured out and has the research to back it up. Instead, I speak to you as my peer. Chances are, if you're experiencing it, I've had similar experiences, too. Throughout my years in leadership, I am continually reminded of the power of vulnerability. While our differences are many, our similarities are what brought you to this book.

With that in mind, explain to your leadership team why you are choosing not to email them in the evenings. Admit to your staff that, as much as you want to support every single student, there is an important reason why they won't see you at some events during the year. Then, with love and respect for those closest to you, train your inner circle to follow Aaron's example of accountability. Practicing caring accountability for those around you and regularly inviting their honest feedback will not just sustain you as a leader but fundamentally alter the culture of your organization.

When the well-being of one another is paramount, even to the point of respectful accountability, genuine care becomes a common thread throughout your school. Without this step, it is easy to give lip-service to balance without ever changing practice or organizational culture. At the end of my time speaking with the leaders who were crumbling under the pace of their unsustainable expectations, one thing was clear: They may have been giving their all to those they led, but they were not giving their best.

Conclusion

Over the next few chapters, this book walks you through ways you can be your very best professionally without sacrificing yourself. However, an imbalanced, hectic professional life will threaten everything that comes later. This is why balance—the psychology behind it and prioritizing it in your life as a leader—is the starting point for this book. I hope you are beginning to see this is a book focused on being vulnerable and real. As you read about my personal experiences, unfolding chapter by chapter, you will discover the things I have needed at different stages of my leadership journey.

I hope you have seen yourself in some way in this chapter. Much like the progression from fear to self-sacrifice, the behaviors explored in further chapters may fall victim to the assumptions controlled by fear if you allow them to. Balance is more than self-care. It's not just about doing things you like. Instead, it is how you allow yourself to thrive—personally, yes, but professionally too. If you want to be a great leader, finding balance allows you to give those you lead the very best you possible.

CHAPTER 2

Making Time for Physical Wellness

"Like I was drowning." These were the only words I could find to explain my feelings to my wife as she worriedly sat on the bed holding my hand. As I lay covered in sweat and aching from my most recent episode, she explained the events of the last several days as if they were part of an eerie bedtime story I was hearing for the very first time. In response to the fresh panic in my eyes, she paused to collect herself before explaining that she had told me all these things several times over the last week.

My time as Aaron's assistant principal was short-lived. It was easily the most fun I ever had in a job, but it was there and gone. An elementary principal in our district left, and I was the person our district intended to take his place. "Ignorance" does not really do justice to the skill set I brought to this campus; I knew nothing about the elementary curriculum and had no experience with elementary students. My new assistant principal, Faith, was everything I wasn't. A former instructional coach, an expert in curriculum, and the walking definition of an instructional leader; her skill set immediately intimidated me. I wrestled daily with the feeling that I had nothing to offer, yet she was quite literally an expert. I couldn't shake the thought that our district should have made her our leader. This was only amplified by every perceived weakness I found in myself. For the first time since my first years in the classroom, I felt completely inadequate.

I shoved aside everything I learned from Aaron about balance and prioritization. I had to learn and learn fast. I decided I had to be at the school every waking hour, regardless of what it cost me. I was willing to do whatever it took to ensure the school didn't fail, especially because of me. Every chance I could, I sacrificed my personal life to show others I could provide value for them. Internally, I felt inadequate and unworthy. Externally, I was giving and giving. I was the first one to arrive and the last to leave. I worked well into the night, slept fitfully, ate only occasionally, guzzled caffeine, and did my best to pass as a polished leader.

On the night of the first parent-teacher conference of the year, my assistant principal found me on the floor of my office amid what would become the first of several seizures I would experience over the next ten days. Two hospital visits, several high-powered medications, and an entire week later, I found myself in bed, covered in sweat, aching and struggling to understand what was happening and why I couldn't remember any of it. That week was when I would hear my neurologist speak the words that became the foundation of this chapter: "Josh, the brain is just an organ. It has limits. When you go past those limits, it will cease to function."

It was the experience of going through these seizures and physical complications that first prompted me to study other leaders across my state. Later, when I read responses and listened to stories from hundreds of practicing leaders throughout Arkansas, one thing became clear: Without balance, physical wellness was often one of the first things to go for practicing educational leaders.

Physical wellness can be a touchy subject. Each of us brings our own bias toward physical health, and we may even harbor unfair self-images. This chapter is not about having the "perfect" body or being hyper-diligent in how and what we eat. Instead, the goal is to bring attention to the fact that when our most fundamental human elements are denied, we have little chance to be our best in the complex role of educational leader. Physical wellness is the physiological foundation on which we build our professional and personal lives. Not unlike a toddler, a sleep-deprived, hungry, thirsty leader is much more likely to revert to their most raw emotional state. If we approach our emotions and behaviors as the function of our brains, then physical wellness is less about body image or perception than about physically setting ourselves up to succeed.

About Physical Wellness

Consider the stories shared in the first chapter. The leaders in the first group were characteristically sacrificial. They found themselves living hurried, imbalanced lives due, at least in part, to meeting the needs of everyone else. When the cost of their professional lives began to overwhelm them, there was little chance they would ask their loved ones to sacrifice more time with them so they could head to the gym or go for a run. When their day was hectic, these leaders would never dream of taking time for a mental break or even to stop and eat a peaceful lunch. The basic physiological needs at the foundation of physical wellness seemed frivolous and selfish. One leader said:

> I put the kids first, I think, by any means necessary. It's going to be whatever it takes. And if that means I don't eat lunch, or I don't eat whatever, I'm going to do whatever it takes, even if I am neglecting myself. (as cited in Ray, 2019, p. 117)

Another leader talked about unhealthy eating habits:

> I do not eat regularly, and when I get the chance to eat, it is typically a "comfort" food rather than a healthy option. I love to cook, and I like healthy food, but cheese-its, popcorn, and wine are often "dinner" even if I didn't eat lunch that day. (as cited in Ray, 2019, p. 103)

Of all the quotes from leaders expressing how their basic physical needs were impacted, few quotes summed up the collective experiences of the first group better than one from a young leader in her third year of being an administrator:

> Depending on the week, eating out is faster than cooking and cleaning up. There are night-time meetings that interfere with family time. Getting a good night's sleep is frequently interrupted by planning for the next day, reliving the stressful situations of the day, remembering things to put on the to-do list, and second-guessing decisions. (as cited in Ray, 2019, p. 103)

Other sentiments I heard include:

- "I had to double my blood pressure prescription yesterday" (as cited in Ray, 2019, p. 114).
- "I'm on three blood pressure pills a day (since) becoming a principal" (as cited in Ray, 2019, p. 114).
- "Over the course of four or five years, my weight grew from about 225 [pounds] to over 300 [pounds]" (as cited in Ray, 2019, p. 115).
- "I know I'm not getting enough sleep because . . . I wake like with these worries that I've forgotten to do something and then I can't go back to sleep. So, I know . . . I'm not making good decisions during the day because I'm sleep deprived" (as cited in Ray, 2019, p. 115).

These devoted leaders, caring to the point of sacrifice, shared more than imbalance. They were united in feeling incapable of meeting their most basic human needs.

I remember vividly the self-care movement that swept the field of education following the Covid-19 pandemic. Schools across North America were forced to daily ask teachers to do new things no one could have imagined being part of the job only months previously. Innovation fatigue, burnout, and frustration quickly became characteristics of educators regardless of state, province, or district. Worried teachers were approaching a breaking point, and many districts brought yet another area of growth to their teachers: self-care. The intentions were undoubtedly good, but this approach sent some unintended messages to educators.

First, there was an overemphasis on individual responsibility. Teachers felt overwhelmed and unprepared for the challenges they could have never imagined. While most wouldn't argue that self-care was important, it was easy to misinterpret this as one more thing on their plate. This was exacerbated when teachers found a way to incorporate some self-care practices only to feel the increasing complexity of their new reality continually shift around them. The "Band-Aid approach" of self-care felt laughably inadequate for teachers' needs during this time.

Finally, teachers, like much of the rest of the world, experienced deep trauma during the pandemic. Educators who had dedicated their lives to serving students had a feeling of moral injury attached to being unable to help the students they served. While self-care was never intended to be an answer to such a weighty experience, teachers could easily mistake self-care as a weak attempt at trying to trivialize the professional trauma many were experiencing (Johnson, 2022). These sentiments seemed to echo among the leaders who were characteristically unbalanced in my study. They knew the difference between healthy choices and unhealthy choices. However, they expressed feeling incapable of juggling these practices along with their already overburdened schedule of responsibilities (Ray, 2019).

On the other hand, the second group—leaders who expressed finding balance in their lives—had some measure of physiological security. I don't mean to suggest that they were all in impeccable physical condition. However, they had learned that, similar to their need for balance, prioritizing some of their most basic physiological needs was not a luxury but a necessity. One leader stated:

> I will, as a person, completely fall apart without these three. And so, one of them is sleep. I require a lot of sleep. My husband and I joked about that when we first got married. He requires less sleep than I do on a daily basis, and so sleep is a big one for me. My nutrition is big. I have to be very careful about—well, not careful, but I should be mindful. I function a whole lot better when I'm getting adequate food. And then my third one is time with my loved ones. I will just completely be ineffective as a leader and as a human being if I am not getting all three of those things on a daily basis. (as cited in Ray, 2019, p. 111)

In many of their comments, these leaders showed little distinction between physical health and balance. They reflected on the importance of "'actively valuing self-care at work with my staff,' 'actively valuing professional and personal growth,' 'teaching self-awareness and stress recognition to our staff,' and 'leaving the management things for tomorrow'" (as cited in Ray, 2019, pp. 111–112). A new leader expressed lessons learned from her first year:

> I've tried to make some better boundaries after the first year. And I've tried to be very present wherever I am, so when that's at work, I am very focused and work very hard. And then when it's time to shut it off and go home, I try very hard to shut it off and go home. And then actually be present when I'm at home, not just physically be there. (second-year administrator, personal communication, October 14, 2018)

She went on to suggest her ability to be present at home went past her emotional health:

> We have started prioritizing family dinners where I can cook healthy food for our entire family. I learned that my best sleep seemed to be happening right after I read a book I was engrossed in. Bedtime reading became part of the family ritual for everyone in our family. We were spending time together, relaxing, and I was sleeping so much better. (second-year administrator, personal communication, October 14, 2018)

Like their approach to balance, these leaders experienced a similar progression of recognition, self-awareness, communicated limits, and accountability in their physical health that I explored in chapter 1 (page 7). With the help of loved ones, they saw areas where their most basic physiological needs were suffering, took the time to recognize and prioritize which areas they wanted to focus on, communicated how they intended to adjust, and held themselves accountable.

Physical Wellness and Decision Making

Finding the balance described in chapter 1 allows us to focus on and solidify our most basic physical wellness routines. My colleagues Timothy D. Kanold and Tina H. Boogren (2022) suggest placing a portion of our daily focus on attending to sleep, hydration, and nutrition.

Attending to these basic physiological needs brings wellness and strength while boosting us professionally and personally. Not coincidentally, these three basic elements were among the ones most often noted among leaders in my study; they are powerful, approachable means of improving both personal and professional effectiveness.

Despite being a highly educated, driven professional and school leader, it's possible your knowledge of what you need to be healthy has not been translated into daily practice in your personal or professional life. The goal of this chapter is to show how care in the basic physical wellness areas of sleep, hydration, and nutrition not only will make you feel better, but can also help you be a better decision maker in your leadership role.

Consider your decisions and behaviors as the function of an organ—the brain—and how our most basic physiological wellness routines could positively or negatively affect the neurological function most often associated with our personalities or character. Like other organs in the body, our habits impact our brain's physical function. Throughout our lives, we have heard the impacts of smoking on the lungs, drinking on the liver, and saturated fats on the heart. For some reason, the brain (the organ that literally runs the functions of our entire physical body) doesn't get the same focus as others. Our basic physiological well-being impacts how we behave, how we make decisions, and how we lead.

The average adult makes at least 35,000 decisions every day (Hoomans, 2015). If you have ever wondered why you sink into a recliner at the end of the day, unsure you'll be able to get yourself back up again, this may be part of the reason! For leaders, our decisions are often not easy. To understand how our basic physical health impacts us, we must understand how we make decisions as leaders.

Joshua Greene and Joseph Paxton (2009) compare the "behind the scenes" of our decision making to a camera. We have an automatic, "point and shoot" function in which emotions influence us into quick decisions. If someone has ever made a request that you immediately recoiled from and, without even thinking about it, snipped an emotional "no way" instead of hearing them out, you've experienced an emotional point-and-shoot decision. That is not to say these decisions are always negative. For instance, if you have ever had someone recommend a small fundraiser to support a staff member going through a time of need, you likely responded almost immediately with an "absolutely." In both cases, the emotion behind the decision was strong enough that you made the decision quickly and decisively without much mental strain or consideration.

However, much like a photographer judging the lighting, choosing the correct lens, and adjusting the camera settings to be just right, we also have a more deliberate, time-consuming way of making decisions. For example, when someone proposes a substantial change to the master schedule or asks you to weigh in on a particularly difficult situation, you take a much different approach. These decisions take effort, time, and a willingness to think through all the possible ramifications. They are not point-and-shoot decisions.

Interestingly, these two ways of forming decisions are often in competition at the most challenging moments (Greene, 2014). Greene (2014) writes that when they compete, it takes a great deal of effort for the more logical decision-making process to win out. When our brain can "point and shoot," it is much easier than all the effort it would take to set up the camera and the surroundings to get the photo just right.

Jonathan Haidt (2006) describes these two ways of making decisions in his book *The Happiness Hypothesis* using the analogy of riding a massive elephant. The rider, significantly smaller than the elephant, can control and direct the animal. However, if the elephant chooses to go rogue from the direction of the much smaller rider, there is little the rider can do to regain control. In this metaphor, the massive elephant is our emotional, automatic approach to making decisions, and the rider is the meticulous guide trying to keep our emotional responses in check.

An example of this in action comes from an often-cited consumer research study conducted in 1999 (Shiv & Fedorikhin, 1999). The participants in the study were asked to remember a number. One-half of the participants were asked to memorize a two-digit number, while the other half were asked to memorize a seven-digit number. With their number assigned, participants were to walk down a hallway to a separate room for an interview. It was casually mentioned that there was a snack cart on the way, and they were welcome to help themselves. On the cart were two choices—chocolate cake and fruit salad. Those asked to remember the two-digit number selected the fruit salad in equal proportion to the chocolate cake. Their seven-digit counterparts overwhelmingly chose the chocolate cake. It was clear for those struggling to remember the much larger number that when given yet another choice, the easier, automatic, and in this case, more impulsive, unhealthy choice won out (Shiv & Fedorikhin, 1999). The reason for taking the time to explain this decision-making process is simple: Physiological health and decisions are powerfully linked. When the brain is overburdened or deprived of the most fundamental things it needs to be healthy, people are significantly more likely to point and shoot or toss the rider and run.

Sleep

Early in my career, my colleague and his wife were blessed with twins. On his first day back at work, I strode into the office, ready to start the day, only to find him sitting hunched over, large dark circles under his bloodshot eyes, a skin tone more closely resembling a ghost than his own, and grasping a cup of coffee like his life depended on it. A few years later, my wife and I left the hospital with a healthy newborn baby boy, thinking, "Did they just send us home with this baby?!" With every coo and gurgle, we sprang into action, like sleep-deprived zombies, with a singular purpose in life. I don't remember a single thing that was happening at work or in the outside world during that time. I wasn't worried about what I ate or drank or what was happening around me. I fell asleep in the middle of the bedroom floor, in the shower, and even once standing at the counter preparing a bottle in the kitchen. We were emotional, irrational, and quick-tempered, but at the root of it all, we were simply exhausted.

Sleep deprivation happens when our bodies are denied the sleep necessary to be our best. Traditionally, sleep deprivation was studied through entire sleepless nights or even several days of sleeplessness in a row. Whether a single sleepless night or multiple nights in a row, the impacts of sleep deprivation on our bodies include decreased psychomotor response times, decreased performance in things that require intense focus, a decline in short-term and working memory, and limitations to our ability to learn new things (Goel, Rao, Durmer, & Dinges, 2009). It doesn't take multiple sleepless nights to influence our cognition and behavior. Research shows that even a single night of sleep deprivation can negatively impact brain function (ScienceDaily, 2023).

When we are sleep-deprived, we are more likely to be impulsive and emotional and much less likely to meticulously analyze a situation to make a thoughtful decision. To use Haidt's (2006) analogy of decision making, the rider is asleep atop the elephant. The elephant is in complete control. When we are sleep deprived, it's more difficult to make subtle emotional evaluations or navigate complex social situations (Tempesta et al., 2010).

In a study comparing sleep-deprived drivers with those whose blood alcohol content was above the legal limit, the results suggested sleep deprivation impaired driving even more than being drunk (Lowrie & Brownlow, 2020). Furthermore, the effects of sleep deprivation even include a diminished ability to act ethically (Yang & Raine, 2009). Imagine a leader whose behavior was defined by these qualities (unable to learn new things, impulsive, quick to react, unable to follow social cues, and unethical). Many of us would automatically consider this a bad leader, or worse, a bad person. However, those same behaviors that would disqualify someone as a leader can be linked to a lack of sleep.

The examples at the beginning of this section were about the sleep deprivation parents of newborns often experience, but for most of us, it's unlikely that we regularly go without any sleep for entire nights at a time. During the regular day-to-day of our lives, we are much more likely to be impacted by *partial sleep restriction*, meaning we get less than enough sleep for several consecutive nights. When we regularly get less than enough sleep, we become so accustomed to the negative effects that it becomes hard to even recognize our need for more rest (Colten & Altevogt, 2006; Fenn, 2023). Also, unlike a single sleepless night, it could be even harder to cognitively overcome the effects of partial sleep restriction without multiple consecutive nights of adequate rest (Colten & Altevogt, 2006; Fenn, 2023). Have you ever found your body needing to "catch up" after several short nights of sleep only to still feel depleted? If so, you likely experienced the effects of partial sleep restriction.

In my study of leaders, sleep was clearly an issue (Ray, 2019). Many leaders recognized this as one of the most important physiological needs they struggled to meet. Nearly one in five of the hundreds of leaders I studied reported getting six or fewer hours of sleep nightly. The vast majority (nearly 80 percent) reported they struggled to fall asleep at least one night per week, and at least three nights per week, they woke up multiple times during the night (Ray, 2019).

Imagine the implications this poses for schools. Most schools in my study were led by sleep-deprived leaders, many of whom experienced the complicated challenges of partial sleep restriction. This means they had likely begun to become accustomed to their sleep-deprived state with little recognition of the impact it had on their performance. All the while, whether they realized it or not, their ability to think critically, navigate emotionally complex situations, and potentially even make ethical decisions could have been severely limited. Regardless of the situation they faced, they found themselves less likely to find success because of the cognitive difficulties they unknowingly struggled to overcome.

Hydration

In our house, there is a corner cabinet. If you open this cabinet, you do so at your own risk. Huge reusable water bottles in every possible color, with some even having markings to track water consumption throughout the day, are stacked haphazardly next to a random assortment of mismatched lids. Each jug or bottle represents a trip we took or a sale we found. They also represent a recurring attempt to drink more water. You may not have a cabinet like this, but I bet you can probably relate.

I say this because each August, in schools across America, teachers come back from summer or holiday breaks armed with similar huge new water bottles and a plan to stay hydrated. Within the first few weeks of school, however, many of these same teachers, like me, find themselves trading water for soda or coffee to make it through the day. What we may not realize is that our dependence on diuretic, caffeinated drinks that can initiate (or worsen) dehydration often begins with a lack of energy that rehydration could solve.

We know that staying hydrated is important, but it may not receive the attention or priority in our lives it deserves. Ask a group of principals how many of them need their coffee in the morning, and you'll see a prioritized need. Ask the same group how many take the time to make sure they drink enough water, and the results will be very different.

Hydration impacts cognitive performance (Nishi et al., 2023), mood, and energy levels (Occupational Safety and Health Administration, n.d.). In a study of driving and the effects of dehydration, those who were dehydrated committed several more driving errors compared to a control group and drove similarly to someone driving while exceeding the legal blood alcohol concentration level (Watson, Whale, Mears, Reyner, & Maughan, 2015). Just like when we are sleep deprived, being dehydrated makes us much more emotional, quicker to make rash decisions, fatigued, and less happy overall. Something as simple as not drinking enough water tips the scales unnecessarily to the point where we find ourselves struggling to keep the raging, emotional elephant in check.

Also, like the effects of partial sleep restriction, we can easily become accustomed to the feelings of dehydration and not recognize our need for water. The good news is that, unlike changing our eating or sleep habits, drinking enough water is, for most of us, as easy as simply having it available. We just need to see it as a priority that makes us better for those we love and lead.

In my study of practicing leaders, nearly 80 percent reported having fewer than eight glasses of water each day (Ray, 2019). Remember earlier when I said leaders love coffee? I found more than a third (36 percent) of the leaders I studied have three or more diuretic, caffeinated beverages daily, while less than 10 percent said they could make it through the day without caffeine. As I said previously, very few leaders see the need for change in this area of their lives. In a group of more than five hundred leaders, only 3.6 percent categorized themselves as dehydrated, and 63.3 percent considered themselves to be at least adequately hydrated (Ray, 2019). This stands in stark contrast with the fact that more than 80 percent were getting less than eight cups of water daily.

Similar to partial sleep restriction, we become accustomed to operating in a state of dehydration and get used to this lifestyle quickly. We just get used to the fact that our brains are groggy and our emotions are high instead of recognizing a negative change in how we feel. If dehydration can impair us so profoundly that we perform similarly to someone drunk behind the wheel of a vehicle, what could this mean for our schools? As leaders, we constantly find ourselves in positions where we must make the choice to accept the automatic, emotional responses that are so easily triggered (elephant) or whether we will make the effort to be deliberately methodical (rider).

Will drinking enough water *ensure* you are more likely to choose the more controlled approach to the challenges of your day? Of course not. That said, it's an easy way to take a step toward being our best as leaders and human beings. Ultimately, the plan is simple. As my friend Tina Boogren would say, "Drink the stupid water"

(T. Boogren, personal communication, February 3, 2003). It's easy, it's free, and you'll be better for it.

Nutrition

"Hey babe . . . I'm planning on making dinner soon." I turned to see a look on my wife's face signaling equal parts shock and disgust. It was Thursday of a particularly crazy week. Only thirty minutes earlier, I had shuffled my haggard self into the house from the garage while seriously questioning how early was too early to go to bed. After realizing 5:30 p.m. was probably a little on the early side, I sank heavily into the recliner in the hope I wouldn't have to move for a while.

The moment I sat down, my stomach started a series of monster-like groans causing me to do a quick mental recap of the last couple of days. I took my two young sons to work with me, and getting out of the house every morning felt like being in a high-stakes game show competition. Yesterday had been especially fun when my oldest took no less than three wardrobe changes to find the look that would impress the middle school critics. There was no time whatsoever for breakfast. Work had been so crazy that I hadn't even noticed that I never stopped to have lunch. On top of that, Wednesday evening was spent at a basketball tournament about three hours out of town. I meant to get something to eat at the games, but I had no cash and then just wanted to get back home afterward.

No wonder I was hungry—I hadn't eaten in two days! Somewhere in this realization, I found myself in the kitchen, refrigerator door still ajar, dipping tortilla chips into a jar of salsa like it was my last meal on earth. Of course, this would be the moment my wife would end her daily afternoon workout only to find her "for better or worse" eating chips and salsa from an open refrigerator like a desperate college kid.

Later in my career, as a high school principal, my nutrition was a mess. Eating had become a cross between necessity and comfort. Much like the story of the salsa jar, I regularly found myself at the end of the day binge eating to satisfy hunger I was ignoring with food that gave me comfort rather than energy. Throughout this time, I was gaining weight at an alarming pace, feeling terrible, and rarely considering that my nutritional habits had any bearing on my ability to be my best for those I loved and led.

Leaders in my study described similar experiences. Eighty-seven percent said they missed lunch at least once during the work week. Two in five of them suggested they missed lunch three or more days a week, which significantly raises the chances these leaders could have gone an entire day without breakfast or lunch. There were twice as many leaders more than fifteen pounds overweight than those near their ideal weight.

More than one-third of the leaders in our study (35.5 percent) perceived themselves to be more than thirty pounds above their ideal weight. Of the over five hundred leaders studied, a tiny 8.3 percent classified themselves as being at their ideal weight, meaning that an overwhelming majority (91.7 percent) felt their body composition was above what they considered ideal (Ray, 2019).

Of all three elements of physical health, nutrition likely holds the greatest stigma. The goal of this section, much like the other two, is not to judge or cast shame. I won't advocate for going on a diet or trying to lose weight. That simply isn't the point. Instead, we are better as leaders when we understand the impact of what we eat on our ability to lead.

In his groundbreaking book *Thinking, Fast and Slow*, Daniel Kahneman (2011) presents decision making and thinking in fascinating ways, paying special attention to the outside influences on our thinking that many either take for granted or never even acknowledge. One such influence on our thinking and personalities is eating. One of his most famous examples is a study of Israeli judges and their judgments on requests for parole (Kahneman, 2011). Kahneman (2011) finds the number of granted requests for parole significantly peaks immediately following the judges' lunch. He suggests that hungry judges give less consideration to the case details and, therefore, choose the safe position of denying the parole request.

This same effect also occurred in a study of Muslim countries during Ramadan. As practicing Muslims in these countries fasted as part of their religious traditions, stock market volatility sharply declined (Hunter, 2013). Like the judges, fasting Muslims were much more conservative in their decisions. Like sleep and hydration, when our nutritional health is out of whack, the brain focuses primarily on solving this fundamental physiological problem instead of the more complex elements of professional leadership.

Kahneman's (2011) work demonstrates that nutrition is more than just what we eat; it has a significant impact on how we feel. If I'm honest, food for me was often either a necessity or a splurge. I never stopped to think about the effect nutrition (or lack thereof) was having on how I felt and functioned both in my personal life and as a leader. One of the changes I have made is to become more mindful about nutrition, so I provided a tool to help you do this as well.

You can use figure 2.1 to chart what you eat and drink and to reflect in the moment on how the way you fuel yourself makes you feel. This mindful approach helps make hydration and nutrition a pursuit of feeling well instead of yet another task on our to-do list.

		Breakfast	Lunch	Dinner	Snacks
Monday	Food and Drink				
	How I Felt	Before: During: After:	Before: During: After:	Before: During: After:	Before: During: After:
Tuesday	Food and Drink				
	How I Felt	Before: During: After:	Before: During: After:	Before: During: After:	Before: During: After:
Wednesday	Food and Drink				
	How I Felt	Before: During: After:	Before: During: After:	Before: During: After:	Before: During: After:
Thursday	Food and Drink				
	How I Felt	Before: During: After:	Before: During: After:	Before: During: After:	Before: During: After:
Friday	Food and Drink				
	How I Felt	Before: During: After:	Before: During: After:	Before: During: After:	Before: During: After:
Saturday	Food and Drink				
	How I Felt	Before: During: After:	Before: During: After:	Before: During: After:	Before: During: After:
Sunday	Food and Drink				
	How I Felt	Before: During: After:	Before: During: After:	Before: During: After:	Before: During: After:

Source: Boogren, 2020, pp. 15–16.

Figure 2.1: Food journal.

*Visit **go.SolutionTree.com/educatorwellness** for a free reproducible version of this figure.*

Physical Wellness as a Priority

When I originally set out to write this book, I intended to place this chapter first. However, my wife wisely reminded me that without balance, discussed in chapter 1 (page 7), physical wellness is unsustainable. We do not set out to be exhausted, dehydrated, or malnourished. However, a hurried life quickly makes even the most basic wellness routines seem frivolous or impossible. When stress consumes us, it doesn't matter what time we go to bed. We struggle to turn off our brains and wrestle with an inability to relax.

Staying hydrated isn't normally a challenge, but with our incredibly full plates, it is difficult to be aware of the impact that just getting enough water has on our ability to be our best. Finally, none of us wants to have poor eating habits, but on our third consecutive night away from home at a ballgame or in the crush of the week before testing, what we eat falls incredibly low on the priority list. Instead, it's much easier to eat when and what is convenient, and we often reach for things that give us comfort instead of what gives us healthy energy.

If you can relate to these experiences, I suggest first taking the time to better understand your state of basic physical wellness. My friends Kanold and Boogren (2022) have some great tools in their book *Educator Wellness* that can help you with this. Figure 2.2 is a physical wellness self-rating tool from that book. It can help you get out of survival mode and take a moment to consider what you eat and drink, how you move, and how you sleep. This also gives you a great starting place to begin making small changes to move toward more healthy habits and improve your overall wellness.

Now, stop and reflect on your current level of physical wellness. Record your thoughts in a notebook or journal.

Stop and Reflect: What Is Your Level of Physical Wellness?

Take a moment to think about your basic physical wellness. What do your results from figures 2.1 (page 43) and 2.2 show you? Is your brain operating at peak capacity, or can your decisions be compromised by your fundamental physical needs? How hydrated are you daily? Do your sleep habits allow you to be your best? Are your nutritional habits fueling you or draining you?

Record your thoughts before you continue reading.

Remember, the goal of this book is not judgment or guilt. Instead, there is a chance that with some recognition and minor changes, you could improve your well-being, performance, and overall fulfillment.

Physical Wellness Dimension		
Food routines: Consider what and when you eat and drink and how well you hydrate during the day.	**Movement routines:** Consider what, when, and how well you move during the day.	**Sleep routines:** Consider how much sleep and rest you get during each twenty-four-hour cycle.
☐ I monitor my food choices most days. ☐ My food choices energize me. ☐ I stay hydrated throughout the day. ☐ I take time to eat breakfast and lunch during my workday. ☐ I am able to eat without distractions. ☐ I monitor how my food choices impact my mood.	☐ I monitor how much I sit or stand each day. ☐ I monitor my number of steps during the day. ☐ I monitor how my movement impacts my mood. ☐ I feel energized most days. ☐ I take brain breaks during my day (perhaps with students). ☐ I practice movement routines with my colleagues or students.	☐ I monitor the hourly amount of my daily sleep. ☐ I feel rested most days when at work. ☐ My sleep positively impacts my mood and behavior. ☐ I use a common daily sleep routine. ☐ I take time to rest during the day without guilt. ☐ I support students or colleagues who may not be getting enough sleep.
1　2　3　4	1　2　3　4	1　2　3　4
Self-Rating: 1 = Beginning; 2 = Implementing; 3 = Embracing; 4 = Modeling		

Self-Reflecting Plan	
Of these three physical wellness routines:	
. . . which routine is your greatest strength, and why?	. . . which routine most needs your attention, and why?

Source: Adapted from Kanold & Boogren, 2022.

Figure 2.2: Educator wellness self-rating and reflection—Physical wellness routines.

*Visit **go.SolutionTree.com/educatorwellness** for a free reproducible version of this figure.*

Strategies to Improve Physical Wellness

My story is dramatic. Not everyone reaches a physical breaking point, but across my state, it was clear there were cracks in the physical foundations of many practicing leaders. Thankfully, this isn't the whole story! The hope of this chapter is that prioritizing these three universal areas of basic well-being can bring you health, joy, and impact. The following are three strategies to help you grow in your physical wellness.

Small Sleep Changes for Big Results

Sleep is different for everyone. Some of us struggle to fall asleep, while others struggle to stay asleep. Some nap easily on the weekends, while others sleep in on weekend mornings to get caught up. There are a few things we can do that universally help with sleep, though.

1. **Limit your blue light exposure close to bedtime:** This simple change has been shown to improve sleep quality, in both the time it takes us to fall asleep and our ability to sleep longer (Silvani, Werder, & Perret, 2022). Many people spend their last wakeful hours engaging with their phone or, even worse, checking email or messages. I often found myself seeking a distraction in the evenings, trying to take my mind off work until I began to feel sleepy. Admittedly, my phone was the initial choice, scrolling and swiping until I found myself wide awake, well past when I wanted to go to sleep. Instead, the simple change of ending my evenings with a book made a huge difference. There were many nights when I fell asleep with my book on my chest, only a few pages into the chapters I planned to read. This was a far cry from the mindless scrolling that took me hours past my bedtime.

2. **Allow yourself to be unavailable:** As technology advances, we are nearly constantly available. For leaders, this can be a blessing and a curse. The simple fact is that we cannot control what information we receive. It could be 9:45 p.m. when you get an email from an angry parent. After reading the email, a few things are true. First, there is likely very little you can do that late in the evening to solve the issue. Next, you likely will not have a great deal of control over your emotional response to the email. In other words, feelings of anxiety, anger, frustration, or disappointment are likely to follow such an email.

   In this heightened state of emotion, you might experience an adrenaline dump and a racing mind. This is the exact opposite of the ideal state for a good night's sleep. This means not sending emails to others, putting away devices, and maybe even charging phones in a separate room. It is completely OK to share with those you lead that you do not intend to check your email after a certain time at night. Instructing those who typically reach out to limit contact with you to emergencies makes it much easier to "turn off."

3. **Ensure your bedroom is extra dark and make the room slightly cooler:** These are easy changes that have an impact on the quality of sleep (Okamoto-Mizuno & Mizuno, 2012). This research suggests these small changes improve not only our ability to fall asleep but also how deeply we sleep. In other words, something as simple as a cool, dark room might mean the difference between waking up with the alarm or restlessly waking many times during the night.

4. **Take a warm bath or shower (around 92°F to 98°F) one to two hours before bed:** This simple "warm bath effect" theory suggests that taking a warm bath improves sleep quality. The science behind this effect is in the impact it has on our circadian rhythm. When our bodies prepare for sleep, our core body temperature naturally drops. The warm water from a shower or bath essentially "jump starts" this process by increasing blood flow to the skin, which helps the body more effectively release heat (Maeda, Koga, Nonaka, & Higuchi, 2023). Add to this the relaxation impact a hot bath or shower has on the muscles, and we find ourselves physiologically much more prepared for sleep.

5. **Do some physical exercise during the day (just not too near to bedtime) and read in the evening:** These seem like simple activities, but they make a big difference in our mental and physical ability to get good sleep.

6. **Ultimately, one of the best things you can do is establish nighttime routines:** If you have ever tried to put a young child to bed, you know your best chance is to try to stick closely to their nightly routine. For my sons, a bath, a book with mom or dad, and a prayer before bed meant the difference between our normal routine and a late-night visit from a sleepless child. Honestly, adults are just big kids. Routine is calming, comforting, and relaxing. Building routine into our lives helps sleep habits be more consistent. Regardless of your routine, regularity matters. The more we can establish a nightly rhythm and regular sleeping and waking times, the more likely we are to regulate our sleep habits (Grandner, 2022).

I have broken myself of the need to check work emails and other activities while I lie in bed the way I did earlier in my career. This isn't to say that I don't get sucked in every now and then, but what became a habit has been replaced by time with my wife; a hot, relaxing shower; a cool, dark room; and a great book. Each of us is different, so try different things to see what works best for you. None of these things are difficult; they just require some changes to your evening routines. Ultimately, isn't your sleep worth it?

Small Hydration Changes for Big Results

Hydration is one of the most accessible physical wellness routines for an individual to work into their busy day. For many of us, this is as easy as ensuring a habit. Of course, the first and most obvious approach is to find ways to get more water across the course of a day. Consider colleagues you work with who always have a cup or water bottle in hand. Simply making sure you have water with you throughout the course of the day is one of the easiest ways to improve your intake.

However, many of us don't consider the many ways we dehydrate throughout the course of the day. Sometimes, we don't feel thirsty because our intake of highly caffeinated coffee and soft drinks has propped us up throughout the day. However, just because we don't feel thirsty doesn't mean we are hydrated. Many times, as we feel fatigued, we reach for caffeine. Especially when combined with sugar in something like a soft drink, we get a shock to the system that results in a feeling of improvement in the short term, followed by a crash later. This cycle perpetuates over and over as we train our bodies to become addicted to caffeine. Sadly, these feelings of fatigue are impacted by the fact that our body is craving *water*—only to be run through a cycle of diuretic, caffeinated drinks.

I definitely still need my caffeine. In fact, anyone who knows me well knows my love for diet Dr. Pepper. I tried to be the big-water-bottle guy, but that just didn't work for me. The office where I worked had a water filler, though. I'll start the morning with a bottle of water from my refrigerator and try to refill it at least four times before lunch. The reason lunch became important to me was the afternoon crash. As I started doing easy things to get enough water before the afternoon, I found myself with noticeably more energy to finish my day. Ultimately, when I was hydrated, I was better. Not only did I feel better, but I also performed better, and that was important.

So, make water a part of your routine. Keep track of how many times you fill your cup or bottle throughout the day. Find ways to allow competition or peer accountability to push your personal progress (Kanold & Boogren, 2022). These are all simple things, but hydration is not difficult! When we are hydrated, our brain function is higher, our bodies feel less hungry, and we have more energy.

Small Nutritional Changes for Big Results

Small changes in your diet begin with the right state of mind. The goal is not to make yourself feel terrible for eating too much. I remember initially sharing the things I learned through my own wellness journey with other leaders. I felt that because I didn't have a runner's physique, this would somehow disqualify me from helping others. Don't allow yourself to fall victim to the lie that nutrition is solely about appearances. Rather, how can you be intentional with what, when, and how you eat so you can feel and be your very best?

First, consider *what* you eat. Each of us has guilty food pleasures that we go back to time and again. The goal is not to push yourself into some unsustainable diet. Instead, what healthy foods do you enjoy? When you know of a few healthy foods that you really like, it becomes much easier to make them a larger part of your diet (Kanold & Boogren, 2022). It's not a chore or a discipline to eat these foods, and they fill some of your caloric intake while minimizing your hunger at times when you can make worse decisions. Personally, fruit and nuts are my go-to snacks. They never feel like a chore to eat; they help me make sure I don't completely miss eating on a crazy day, and they give me something to look forward to that is healthy.

Next, consider *when* you eat. For many educational leaders, lunch is inconsistent at best. After a long day with no lunch, sometimes no breakfast, and a tired, weakened mind and body, many of us overeat and go for "feel good" foods that don't meet the body's nutritional needs. It may take a little bit of intentionality, but you can improve what and when you eat at the same time. Prepping lunches before the workweek begins means a healthy meal is ready for you. Making a piece of fruit and some granola or an energy bar part of your morning routine is quick and easy. You can develop a habit and start your body in the right place at the beginning of the day.

I wish I was a meal prepper, but I have just never been successful with this. Instead, I make sure to always have lots of healthy snacks in my office. Mixed nuts, healthy meat sticks, and fruit give me things to snack on throughout the day that I can buy all at once and eat throughout the week. They also help curb the ravenous hunger I used to experience at the end of a long day.

Finally, consider *how* you eat. How you eat makes a big difference in your nutritional routines. Often, educational leaders find themselves eating at the convergence of convenience and necessity. For me, this meant overeating junk late in the evenings at ballgames or on the way home. Tired and mentally drained, I reached for unhealthy choices to feel good. Sometimes, this was my first meal of the day. I would hurriedly cram a high-calorie, high-fat meal and physically crash even more. My abundance of healthy snacks makes such a difference. While I may still be hungry if I miss lunch, I can grab a handful of something healthy a few times in the afternoon, so I stay satisfied with healthy energy.

I may struggle to have the chance to sit and have a meal, but I can keep myself from being overly hungry by consuming healthy snacks I enjoy throughout the day. This also gives me a chance to eat periodically throughout the day instead of rushing through a meal. Grabbing fast food on the way to the game meant I was consuming several thousand calories in a hurry before my duties began. However, periodically snacking on healthy things throughout the day levels my metabolism, gives me steady energy, and keeps me from a quick caloric binge that results in an energy crash.

Conclusion

Before this chapter ends, I want to remind you that the goal is not to add to your incredibly full plate. I encourage you as a leader not to approach your physical wellness from the perspective of another to-do list for you and those you lead. Instead, look for ways you can infuse wellness into your professional practice for the purpose of being your best, professionally and personally. There are so many approaches to this! Don't try to completely change your routine if, like me, you're not a meal prepper. Just make sure you have water and enough healthy snacks to make it through the day feeling better than you would have otherwise. Start small in ways that work for you. No one is suggesting you sign up for a decathlon. By simply getting some more water, though, you'll be more cognitively sound and feel better.

The promise of this book is that there are simple ways to make your life more fulfilling while making you even better at your job. Remember that you at your best for eight hours is worth more than a compromised you for ten. Wellness is not a destination. Instead, like my choice to watch a television show at night with my wife, there may be fun, easy ways for you to be better. With just a few small changes, you can be more effective, happier, and better for the most important people in your life. It's well worth it!

CHAPTER 3

Being the Leader You Aspire to Be

It was nearly three weeks (after more than twenty seizures) before I was able to return to our elementary campus. Heavily medicated, still somewhat confused, and a physical shell of what I was only a month earlier, I returned to a school that hadn't fallen apart without me. As a young leader, I found myself in a watershed moment. I could continue trying to overcompensate for the things I wasn't, or I could choose to be what I was for our campus. My seizures and time away from school didn't erase my self-doubt, but it did help me recognize that the absence of my unsustainable effort, while hurting me daily, absolutely did not keep the school from thriving while I was gone. I had to decide whether to keep working to exhaustion at overcoming my weaknesses or to begin growing my strengths.

Aaron and his family had been to our home many times during my seizures (none of which I remembered). He knew me well, which meant he knew to check on my wife and boys. On my first week back at school, he asked if I had a few minutes to chat at the end of the day. As I drove across town to the junior high, I was preparing myself for a scolding from my best friend. He knew me well enough to know how I was responding to all this stress; in fact, this had dominated many of our most recent Saturday morning conversations over coffee and cinnamon rolls at the local diner.

Instead, as I walked into his office, he stood up from his desk, engulfed me in a huge hug, and told me how lucky our district was to have me back. As he listed the things he missed when I was gone, he reminded me again and again how great I was with people. Truthfully, I didn't know much more about the junior high school curriculum as his assistant principal than I did then about the elementary school curriculum that threatened to expose me, but it never came up in our conversation. According to him, I could "bring out the best in people" and make them "feel like their contributions were important."

Leaving Aaron's office that day, I realized I had learned yet another incredibly important lesson. My assistant principal, Faith, was incredible. However, all my effort spent trying to overcome not being her was keeping me from being *me*. I could bring out the best in people, I could motivate them, and I could find and develop other leaders throughout our school. Maybe instead of spending so much time trying to be something I wasn't, I could serve our school by being the best version of who I was.

The first two chapters of this book focused on you, *the person*. This was intentional in that your well-being is foundational to your personal and professional performance. As I shift to you, *the leader*, the same psychology and fear behind imbalanced leaders play a major role. For me, imbalance and physical crumbling came out of my feelings of inadequacy. Those feelings were only heightened by my choice to constantly focus on my shortcomings rather than the unique qualities I brought to the role.

I encourage you to try to avoid this trap. Deficiency mindsets lead to imbalance. Imbalance leads to compromise in your personal and, often, physical well-being. However, the impact goes further. Being the leader only you can be, the one you hoped to be when you first took the job, will carry over into every other component of your personal and professional life.

About Being the Leader You Aspire to Be

Think for a moment about when you found out you were getting your current job. Like all of us, there were certainly things you couldn't have anticipated you'd be doing. However, what were the dreams you had for your new role? Did you imagine leading others to be more effective in their instructional practices? Maybe you thought about practical changes you could bring to the role that would improve the professional lives of those you served. Regardless of what it was, you probably entered your current role with excitement for what was possible and possibly even a touch of starry-eyed naivety.

How many of those job duties, the ones you looked so forward to, are part of your daily duties today? The truth is, much like our work-life balance, our roles as leaders can grow out of our control. For many of us, the dreams we have for our roles can easily be pushed aside by a state of hurry and professional survival. We won't ever be able to completely tailor our role to be what we hope. However, as leaders, we should be able to approach our jobs with intention.

To do this, you must first understand who you are and what you bring to the job. Regardless of your professional experience or résumé, you have traits and skills that can have a uniquely powerful impact on those you lead. Next, you should understand what it means to be happy in your role. Somehow, it becomes easy for many of us to think that happiness at work is somehow frivolous. Instead, when you are fulfilled, you are better. Happiness isn't a luxury; it's like a professional growth hormone. Happiness makes us more effective, not the other way around. Last, armed with an understanding of your unique gifts and the elements of your role in which you are most fulfilled, it's time to start budgeting your time. You can either plan your schedule or let it happen to you. Sure, on some days, best-laid plans go out the window. But week after week, with focus and intention, your role can shift from mere survival to purpose, enjoyment, and true impact.

Leadership Traits and Styles

What traits and styles make a great leader? There has been a great deal of research in this area. The trait theory of leadership looks for the type of person who becomes a great leader (Zaccaro, 2007). In 2002, Timothy A. Judge, Joyce E. Bono, Remus Ilies, and Megan W. Gerhardt conducted a meta-study meant to extract all the different characteristics of great leaders. With more than 1,000 initially identified, 83 characteristics were eventually chosen (Judge et al., 2002). Most of us have likely experienced many different traits in great leaders. Some transformational leaders are charismatic, able to rouse others with their vision and words, while others are total introverts who struggle to muster the courage necessary to speak to a roomful of people.

Ultimately, there's no single type of person who makes a great leader. This is important for leaders who struggle with feelings of imposter syndrome. While others may possess leadership qualities we do not, our leadership isn't defined by the absence of any one trait. You may be uniquely gifted at motivating others, leading instructional practice, managing complex systems, or surrounding yourself with great talent. Any one of these traits could be the foundation for an incredibly influential leader, but it is highly unlikely that any one of us possesses them all.

Our goal as leaders should not be to tirelessly pursue the leadership qualities we lack. Instead, we are at our best when we are serving and influencing in areas of our unique strengths and gifts. The job of an educational leader is complex and busy. The difference between living our professional life as an unfulfilled "educational firefighter," constantly rushing to put out fire after fire, or a happy, intentional difference-maker often depends on our ability to know ourselves and prioritize our impact.

In the book *Stronger Together*, Terri L. Martin and Cameron L. Rains (2018) state, "Collaborative leaders are at their best when they know who they are and what they can do" (p. 7). Great leadership is collaborative, but our ability to be our best lies in our ability to understand ourselves, understand the purpose of our organization, what we can bring to those we lead, and what we need from those who lead alongside us.

Leadership styles are as unique as the leaders themselves. Your talents, skills, decisions, and interactions with others all collectively form your leadership style. Matt Gavin (2019) suggests, "A leadership style entails the patterns of behavior that are consistent across how you make decisions, interact with others, and use your time. It's also characterized by how your colleagues would describe their working relationship with you." Gavin (2019) suggests there are three specific leadership styles in which most of us fall: (1) approachable, (2) credible, or (3) aspirational. While you may have characteristics of each of these three styles, you will likely find yourself falling predominately in one of these categories.

Approachable

Leaders defined by their approachability are known for their "authenticity and warmth" (Gavin, 2019). These leaders are most typified by their strong emotional intelligence. For the sake of clarity, "emotional intelligence is the ability to accurately perceive your own and others' emotions; to understand the signals that emotions send about relationships; and to manage your own and others' emotions" (Harvard Business Review Staff, 2004). If you are a leader whose style is typified by this characteristic, people who work with you would likely use words like *supportive*, *encouraging*, *empathetic*, *understanding*, *fair*, and *authentic* to describe you. You would likely be best remembered for your relationships, your ability to connect to those you lead, and your ability to make others feel important.

Credible

Credible leaders impart knowledge and authority and encompass competence, humility, and resolve (Gavin, 2019). Leaders who are primarily known for their credibility are those everyone looks to in times of need. Those you lead trust you, but maybe even more importantly, they trust your decisions. Credible leaders are *tried and true*. They are *battle-tested* and *dependable*. They may not have the level of emotional intelligence of their approachable peers, but their expertise elicits confidence in those they lead. If you are a credible leader, those you lead will comment on your *integrity*, *competence*, *decisiveness*, and *composure*. They may not necessarily feel connected to you, but they trust you because of your track record. They know what you stand for, and they see your calm in the storm.

Aspirational

Aspirational leaders are consumed with a vision of what is possible. Their zeal is contagious and motivational for others. If you are an aspirational leader, you can't help but see the potential in others. Or, as Gavin (2019) writes, "An aspirational leader brings out the best in both themselves and others." You have high expectations, but you also pride yourself in your ability to create a belief in what is possible. Those you lead would describe you as *visionary*, *strategic*, *innovative*, *empowering*, and *authentic*. You believe wholeheartedly in the future you envision, and bringing out the best in others is how you realize the vision together. While people may not feel connected to you in the way they do with an approachable leader, they are inspired by you. Also, you may not provide the comfort of predictability the credible leader offers, but there is an excitement for those who take part in your vision that is hard to ignore.

When we understand our unique leadership strengths and how these strengths can benefit those we lead, we can be intentional in our pursuit of professional fulfillment. It's easy to think of being happy as a fleeting emotion. The challenge with emotions is that they are typically responses to outside stimuli. I encourage you to think less about feelings of happiness and, instead, consider a state of joy. Joy, in contrast to happiness, is a response to internal stimuli. When we professionally focus on areas of meaning and purpose, joy becomes an outflow of our controllable actions instead of an emotional reaction to uncontrollable outside stimuli. Living a purposeful, fulfilling, professional life doesn't mean you won't have bad days. However, when we face difficult times as leaders, being anchored in and focused on our purpose ensures we don't find ourselves adrift and struggling to keep our heads above water.

The Pursuit of Happiness

What does it mean to be happy? What first seems like a simple question can begin to feel complex. Happiness is something all of us long for. We find happiness in those we love, and we find it in things we enjoy. However, when it comes to work, many people find themselves just trying to "make it" to the end of the day or the weekend. Our ability to find happiness inspired the research of then-Harvard student, and later University of Pennsylvania researcher, Matthew A. Killingsworth.

Matthew A. Killingsworth and Daniel T. Gilbert (2010) created an app called Track Your Happiness. They found that happiness is tied closely with fleeting experiences throughout the day, such as who we are with, what we are doing, and what we are experiencing. This is not to say that larger things don't have an impact on our happiness, but our emotional state often reflects the smaller things that become part of the rhythm of our everyday lives.

Their research finds one of the greatest threats to our daily happiness is mind wandering, something so universal to the human experience that many may not often even realize it is happening (Killingsworth & Gilbert, 2010). Killingsworth and Gilbert (2010) say it best when they write, "A human mind is a wandering mind, and a wandering mind is an unhappy mind. The ability to think about what is not happening is a cognitive achievement that comes at an emotional cost" (p. 932).

Among the 650,000 responses they recorded from participants on their app, Killingsworth and Gilbert (2010) found that people reported thinking about something other than what they are doing 47 percent of the time and that their "wandering minds" had a substantially negative effect on their happiness. Even the most mundane, menial tasks were completed with a substantially higher level of fulfillment and happiness when the person reported their mind focused on what they were doing.

Because of the high level of responses in this study, the research team was able to take this information a step further. They write that mind wandering is an effective predictor of happiness. How often our minds leave the present and where they tend to go is a better predictor of our happiness than the activities we are engaged in (Killingsworth & Gilbert, 2010).

As leaders, it can feel like we are in a never-ending battle for our time and focus. Best-laid plans are often derailed by things we can't control or can't account for. Still, it's unlikely for us to completely silence the distractions of educational leadership. As a young leader, I wasn't even sure what I was being distracted from. I knew my weaknesses, worried about how people perceived me, and played a never-ending game of catch-up, all while trying to work hard enough to overcome my feelings of inadequacy. What I needed was purpose and the freedom that comes from knowing who I was as a leader and focusing on being my best.

Leadership Self-Assessment

You may have already begun to see one of the leadership styles from this chapter that most fits your characteristics. However, to understand your leadership style requires self-assessment and input from those you lead. To do this, I suggest considering your leadership styles through three distinct lenses: (1) how you impact others, (2) how you define your role, and (3) what motivates you as a leader.

How You Impact Others

All leaders create an experience for those who experience their leadership. Using Gavin's (2019) three leadership styles, it is not hard to imagine the experience of those working with each type of leader. For those following a leader characterized by their approachability, they would likely feel understood, valued, and heard. Those working with a leader known for their credibility would likely feel security and confidence in their ability to predict the actions of their leader. Finally, those working alongside an aspirational leader would feel motivated, stretched, and inspired. If you want to better understand your style of leadership, look first to the experiences of those you lead.

How You Define Your Role

The next step in assessing your leadership style is to assess how you define your role. The complexity of school leadership means you wear many hats throughout the course of the year. To help simplify finding your definition of leadership, group the functions of your role in two distinct boxes: structural and cultural. A leader's ability to organize resources, design a master schedule, mobilize others, and communicate tasks is paramount to success. These are primarily structural components of leadership. Our ability to invest in others, create common understanding, provide guidance, and grow other leaders are examples of cultural components of leadership. The balance of the cultural and structural tasks we prioritize paints a picture of our purpose as leaders. At the root of our purpose lie the beliefs and motivations that influence our behaviors.

What Motivates You as a Leader

What components of your job do you love the most? What are the things that bring you fulfillment and purpose? All of us experience two types of motivators: (1) external and (2) internal. External motivators include recognition for you or your organization, success when compared to other schools or leaders, professional promotion, and financial incentives. External motivation with those we lead might be someone recognizing our efforts, congratulating us on success, or thanking us for our care for them.

Internal motivators can be influenced by the external. Some leaders want those they lead to like them; others are driven by their effectiveness or efficiency; and some may be motivated by a dream of what is possible. Do you find motivation by helping others feel understood or connected, by making others feel confident in your ability, or by motivating or inspiring them to be something they may have never realized without your leadership? Our internal motivations are fueled by external affirmation. On the other hand, those we lead will experience externally what fuels us internally. Knowing what motivates you can help you find your leadership style and envision the experience of those you lead.

As I considered myself through these lenses, a picture of my leadership style started to form. Those I led valued how I made them feel. They believed I was genuine and cared about them as professionals and people. When I considered how I prioritized the tasks of my job, it was clear I placed a heavy emphasis on the cultural components. I could build a master schedule, but I didn't enjoy doing it. I wanted to be in team meetings with teachers or in the halls with students. I found purpose in how I took care of those I led, and my actions followed suit. I also found that I was deeply motivated by what was possible and my ability to bring out the best in others. I also cared sincerely about what people thought about me as a leader. I knew that not everyone would always love the decisions I had to make, but it mattered to me that everyone knew I cared. I am a textbook approachable leader. While I have components of aspirational leadership, the driving force behind the experiences of those I led, my perception of my purpose, and my deepest motivations came down to my ability to connect with people.

You can use the leadership style assessment in figure 3.1 to discover the unique impact your leadership style brings to your position.

Directions: Choose the number in each row that best describes you. Consider asking others to use this tool to assess your leadership as well.

	1	2	3	Your Trait Number
Impact on Others	Others know you genuinely care. They know you prioritize them as people. You make them feel cared for.	Others trust you in the "storm." They can predict your decisions. You make them feel confident.	Others are inspired by your passion. They know your vision. They feel that you bring out the best in them. You make them feel empowered.	
Your Role Defined	You are drawn to cultural aspects of your job. You find purpose in supporting and protecting those you lead.	You are drawn to structural aspects of your job. You find purpose when developing systems or structures and when solving problems or completing tasks.	You love to multiply the strengths of others. Your purpose for your work lies in helping others find the untapped abilities they may not have known otherwise.	
Your Motivations	You are motivated by the power of the relationships you enjoy. You pride yourself in supporting those you lead and being there when they need you.	You are motivated by technical challenges. Tackling a difficult task is motivating and draws your attention. You pride yourself in your ability to get the job done and figure out what others cannot.	You are motivated by empowering others. You see everyone's potential and are motivated to bring it out in them. You pride yourself in your ability to cast a vision and rally your troops.	

Figure 3.1: Leadership style assessment.

*Visit **go.SolutionTree.com/educatorwellness** for a free reproducible version of this figure.*

If you scored more ones, you are an approachable leader. More twos suggest you influence others through your credibility. Finally, if you scored more threes, you are likely an aspirational leader. With this knowledge, you can predict the areas where you will be most impactful for those you lead.

Leadership and Time Priorities

Hopefully, your impact on others, purpose, and motivation are becoming evident to you. This begs the question, "Do you spend your time in these areas, or do you struggle to even operate in your strengths because of the busy nature of your job?" Do you know the times during the day when your influence is most important? Understanding yourself, your leadership impact, and the purpose of your school means little if it does not influence the allocation of your time and influence.

Have you ever started the day with a to-do list only to end the day without a single thing accomplished from that list? Of course, there will inevitably be days like these in educational leadership. The question is whether these days are the rule or the exception to the rule. Unfortunately, many educational leaders find themselves at the mercy of their ability to manage the constant threats to their focus.

Not long ago, a new leader I know experienced something very similar. I will call her Anna. It was an important day on her campus. Anna was welcoming two educational coaches from out of state who were coming to support her and her teachers. Anna knew her strengths as an instructional leader. She was gifted in the classroom and had a desire to bring her instructional expertise to her leadership position. On this day, Anna came to work, excited to take part in a day destined to hit her right in the strengths of her leadership skill set. Before the day had even begun, her plate was full. Student discipline, parent phone calls, communication, and simply surviving the day quickly stole her focus. As she finally climbed out to the other side of the day she never saw coming, the teachers and students were gone, and she had barely even spoken to the two experts she was so excited to learn from.

Anna called me to vent her frustrations. It wasn't until she began to talk about her day that she began to realize the number of things she had prioritized that weren't emergencies. Yes, discipline had to be addressed, but she had others on her team who were even better at handling it than she was. Once Anna went down this road, she fielded several phone calls that others could have handled. She chose to respond to one email only to see another email from a teacher that, once she fully researched and answered him, cost her yet another two hours. No doubt, it was a busy day.

It would have been understandably difficult for Anna to be completely present with her teachers and the experts that day. However, her choice to follow unnecessary trails meant she missed the chance to do what she did best. As Anna talked to me, she recognized her perceived need to finish her checklist caused her to miss a day in which she could have operated with her strengths. What motivations are driving your days? Is there a chance, like Anna, that a subconscious need to clear your inbox or to-do list could overtake your professional purpose?

In his book *Good to Great*, Jim Collins (2001) describes the simplicity of the hedgehog in contrast to the complexity of its predator, the fox. Where the fox is creative and finds many ways to attack its prey, the hedgehog protects itself by doing only one thing incredibly well; it rolls into a spikey ball. In schools, educational leaders face an onslaught of information. Reviewing student data, examining financial information, responding to human resource demands, and communicating with stakeholders are only a few of the things that relentlessly tug at the focus of leaders. Without purposeful intention, professional survival while trying to simply check all the boxes allows little time to lead in our unique purpose.

As Kanold and Boogren (2022) write, "Busy is good; hurried is not so good" (p. 30). Many leaders would say they have great plans but never find the time to start or sustain the plans they envision. On the other hand, purposeful leaders in great companies Collins (2001) referenced (for example, Gillette, Kroger, Walgreens, and so on) navigate the complexity of the job while devoting unwavering focus on what is most important.

Of course, you can't ignore the necessary tasks of your job, but you can prioritize your efforts. Like strengths, we also have weaknesses. In the imbalanced group of leaders I studied, group members had a clear awareness of their weaknesses and made an effort to overcome them. While this may seem noble, it requires a great deal of time and effort. As a result, the unique strengths of their leadership get put on hold while they focus on improving their weaknesses. Sure, they will undoubtedly improve in these areas, but will they ever be as good as someone on their team who is gifted in areas where they are weak?

Unfortunately for so many of us, our perceived need to "take things off the plate" of others means we eat from a jumbled, mismatched plate ourselves. This is distracting and diminishing and denies us the chance to focus on being great at our own "hedgehog concept," the area of focus where we feel the unique combination of passion, impact, and strength (Collins, 2001). This approach places a much higher priority on service and the comfort of others than it does on results. The benefits of this approach to leadership lie in perception and in gratitude for those we serve, but it comes at the cost of our efficiency and impact (Bolman & Deal, 2021).

Strength-Based Leadership

For the imbalanced leaders, the desire to work on their weaknesses originates from the same source of their imbalance—fear. Fear of failure drives us to take a deficiency-focused approach to leadership, constantly overcompensating and overdoing. Thankfully, we don't have to settle for this! The alternate approach is strength-based leadership. Strength-based leaders focus on identifying, developing, and employing their strengths and the strengths of those they lead (Ward, 2018). Instead of the stress and negativity associated with constantly working on individual deficiencies, this approach to leadership shows a positive impact on job satisfaction (Duan, Ho, Tang, Li, & Zhang, 2014), work-related wellness (Meyers & van Woerkom, 2017), and performance (van Woerkom et al., 2016).

These benefits are not difficult to understand. Leaders who can see the strength in themselves understand their greatest contribution to those they serve. With practice, they become great at finding the unique strengths of others and deploying them in their strengths. This is rewarding for those they lead as well as themselves.

The imbalanced leaders in my study felt such pressure to be all things to everyone that they could find no time to be their best. While they felt they were serving those they led, they were unintentionally stealing others' opportunities to contribute their unique strengths to leadership. Like the promise of all the other components of this book, strength-based leadership is not only more effective; it is more fulfilling and sustainable.

Now, stop and reflect on the kind of leader you want to be. Record your thoughts in a notebook or journal.

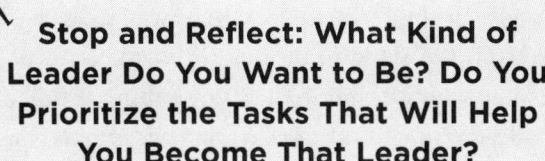

> **Stop and Reflect: What Kind of Leader Do You Want to Be? Do You Prioritize the Tasks That Will Help You Become That Leader?**
>
> Take a moment to think about yourself as a leader. What type of leader do you want to be? Is this reflected in your personal strengths? With this in mind, how are you spending your time? Do you control your schedule, or does it control you? Are you prioritizing the tasks that will make you the leader you aspire to become?
>
> Record your thoughts before you continue reading.

Strategies to Manage Your Time

At this point in the chapter, you should have a better understanding of your leadership style. You should have an idea of what those you lead value in you, understand the purpose of the organization you serve, and realize the importance of prioritizing your time and efforts. Now, it's time to plan your day with all of this in mind.

Put Things on a Calendar

First, you need a plan for the "stuff" of the job. How will you prevent the necessity of task completion from derailing your unique impact? Regulation is the intentional decision to confine certain tasks to a controllable amount of your schedule. For instance, email is a never-ending stream. You could spend twenty-four hours a day trying to stay on top of the wave, or you could simply decide you will set aside a specific time to address emails. Maybe this is first thing in the morning, so you have the rest of the day to respond accordingly. Or maybe you designate a little time in the morning and a little time in the afternoon, so when you leave work at the end of the day, you know what you have accomplished and what you can pick up the next morning.

You will also want to designate specific times for tasks you might otherwise neglect. For example, you might want to ensure you have time to interact with students by scheduling time in the cafeteria during lunch, or you might put times in your calendar to check in with teachers during their planning time. What you regulate depends on your leadership style. If you are motivated by the structural elements of your role, it makes sense to regulate time to ensure you address the cultural side, and vice versa.

Once you've planned times for low-impact tasks that might otherwise have been missed or avoided, you now have the opportunity to prioritize and budget for the most important things. In the elementary school where I served as principal, our teachers had "protected time." This meant that they had blocks of instructional time during the day when the school committed to not pulling a student from instruction for any reason. As a leader, it should not be a luxury to have some protected time of your own. This takes coordination, though. Those who lead with you need to understand how to prioritize this time, recognize their role in helping you protect time to do what is most important, and have a clear definition of what constitutes the type of emergency that requires pulling you from this time.

As a young leader, I had to protect the time out of my office to observe learning. I am naturally a fixer by nature, so I knew that if I did not set aside this time, I would easily get trapped in trying to fix the most immediate problems. This meant I let my leadership team know I would be in classrooms; yes, I would have my cell phone, but it was important I was not disturbed during this time except for very specific circumstances. This meant that parents who called during this time or even came to visit me would hear that I was unavailable for the next hour. Teachers began to recognize that there were times during the day when I was much more difficult to reach.

The message I sent by prioritizing my time was that my presence in classrooms, supporting teachers and student learning, was more important than anyone's perceived need for me to be constantly available. Ultimately, people adapt to the expectations you hold. No one would consciously voice they expect their leader to be immediately available at all times. However, they will look to your practice to determine your purpose. If you put great effort into being constantly available by email, others will develop an expectation based on the habits they've seen. Prioritize your time, protect your priorities, and communicate these things with others.

Conduct a Time Audit

If you are struggling to manage the constant flow of your day, a time audit could help you determine how your time reflects your goals. To conduct an audit, each time you start a new task, write down the starting time as well as the time you finish. Then, consider the priority of this task to your success as a leader and fulfilling your purpose. Figure 3.2 offers a simple tool to help you with this task.

Time Audit

Directions: Use this tool throughout the day to record each task you complete, how long you devote to it, and how important it is in being your best as a leader. Score each task from 1–4 (with 1 being most important and 4 being least important).

Date	Activity	Start Time	End Time	Total Time	Priority Score 1–4

Figure 3.2: Time audit tool.

Visit **go.SolutionTree.com/educatorwellness** *for a free reproducible version of this figure.*

Conducting a time audit will show how you use your time and how you can make small changes to operate more efficiently and purposefully. You may find that your day is spent inefficiently attending to multiple things distractedly, fostering the unhappiness of a wandering mind (Killingsworth & Gilbert, 2010) while never fully accomplishing what you set out to do. Interestingly, simply writing down the start and end times in a time audit can help with this, as you will naturally start to focus more on the task at hand. You may also find that you are not approaching parts of your day purposefully and are, instead, spending large chunks of time responding. This will help you see if your time reflects the importance of the tasks you complete.

These realizations are so freeing for leaders! Before conducting a time audit, you may feel overwhelmed and helpless, but results like these can help you see small tweaks you can make to regulate the less important parts of your jobs. As you consider the importance of the tasks you complete, the Eisenhower Box, shown in figure 3.3, offers a simple means of deciding how to reallocate your time (Clear, n.d.). This tool comes from the genius of five-star general and former president Dwight Eisenhower. He broke down tasks into four distinct categories:

1. Urgent and important (tasks you do immediately)
2. Important but not urgent (tasks to schedule for later)
3. Urgent but not important (tasks to delegate to someone else)
4. Neither urgent nor important (tasks to eliminate; Clear, n.d.)

	URGENT	NOT URGENT
IMPORTANT	**DO** Attend today's meetings. Complete time-sensitive tasks.	**DECIDE** Schedule a time to do it. Go for a walk. Call family or friends.
NOT IMPORTANT	**DELEGATE** Find someone to help you with tasks. Schedule meetings. Organize events.	**DELETE** Scroll through social media. Watch mindless television.

"What is important is seldom urgent and what is urgent is seldom important."

—Dwight Eisenhower, 34th President of the United States (as cited by Covey, 1989, p. 109)

Source: Adapted from Clear, n.d.
Figure 3.3: The Eisenhower Box.

The results from your time audit, considered through the lens of Eisenhower's simple matrix, could help you begin to reclaim the focus of your day. Delegating and deleting tasks means more time for you to devote to your purpose and priorities.

Conclusion

In the first two chapters, we considered balance and how it can impact efficiency, effectiveness, and even physical well-being. For many leaders, a great source of imbalance lies in a perceived inability to control the pace of their job. When the job dictates our priorities and purpose, it could begin to control our time, energy, and well-being. What is encouraging for us as leaders is that the very things that help us regain control also make us more effective and happier in our jobs.

You have a unique set of gifts and style. You work in a unique educational organization. With some intentionality and focus, you could spend your days living professionally in your purpose for the betterment of your school. Take the time to be intentional and be willing to reallocate your time. The promise of this effort is an escape from hurry and the balance, happiness, and influence that comes from leading with purpose.

CHAPTER 4

Leading Change

While it may have taken a physical breakdown, I returned as an elementary principal with newfound direction and a reminder from Aaron of who I was as a leader. We were a school full of professionals who cared deeply about being their best for students, but there were undoubtedly students we weren't reaching. Our campus had received a B on our state report card, which was by no means bad but far from what we were capable of. Our teachers were working incredibly hard individually, but we were not unified in our pursuit of success for every student.

Our campus allowed parents full access to choose their child's teacher. This meant teachers had to compete against each other for the attention of families throughout the community. Our specialized teachers were crumbling under the weight of the number of students they were trying to serve throughout the day. If there were eight workdays per week, they still couldn't have met the needs of these students on their own. This meant we were identifying a disproportionate number of students for special education services because teachers simply couldn't deliver the help their students needed.

Personally, I had come face to face with the ramifications of an imbalanced, unwell lifestyle. This made the strain of those I was leading that much more obvious to me. Change was necessary across the school if we wanted to preserve our teachers and serve our students. With a newfound foundation of balance, a purpose, and a collective vision for our school, I charged headfirst into change with zeal and idyllic excitement. All at once, we had a new master schedule, we removed teacher requests, we upped the rigor of our assessments, and we implemented a new multitiered system of supports. To be clear, there wasn't a single change we made that was bad practice or unnecessary. However, I learned quickly that change, even when purposeful and meaningful, is still difficult.

In just a few weeks, I realized no one was sitting next to me at the building potluck. When I entered the room, people seemed to stop talking. My visions of grandeur, my thought that I would be like the picturesque George Washington, leading his troops across the Delaware, quickly turned into the recognition that leading change, while necessary, was incredibly difficult and lonely. Families and even some teachers were furious with the decision to no longer allow parents to pick their child's teacher.

As we began to change our instructional practices over the next few months, there were tears and emotional outbursts among the staff. I began to worry I had broken our campus. The day after our first interim exam since implementing the changes, I couldn't shake my anxiety. The butterflies in my stomach only intensified when my assistant principal and I got the text from our instructional coaches that the scores were in. We all convened in our conference room to look at them together. Surely, they would be good. We were working so hard, our leaders had endured so much, and our teachers deserved to see success.

Within moments of seeing our instructional coaches' faces, it was clear that the news was not good. Our scores hadn't increased. In fact, despite all our efforts, the interim showed either stagnant scores or some that even went down. We were only months into major change, and this blow made me question everything we had done. My doubts were substantial, and the imposter syndrome raged within me all over again. Were all the changes we made as necessary as we had once felt?

We had a choice to make. Should we continue to endure the anxiety and stress across our campus, or should we just count our losses, admit defeat, and move forward? After all, we weren't a bad school; we just wanted to be better. The rest of the day went by slowly and painfully. I worried the leaders of our school were wrestling with the same doubts. In hindsight, left to myself, I really am not sure how the story would have ended. Thankfully, my colleagues were resolute in their belief in the change we were making. What we were doing was right for our students, but we had to improve our ability to lead the change throughout our staff—and this change had to begin with me.

This recommitment was a turning point for our school's leadership and for me. We continued to grow and change to be our best for our staff. Things were not immediately easier, but with the help of many others, momentum grew, and positive changes emerged. Little by little, we started to experience the victories we dreamed of and saw our staff change. It was not long at all before it felt almost silly that I had even considered abandoning our work, but even then, we could not have imagined the success and recognition in store for our staff and students.

Looking back on this experience, my greatest takeaway is simple: Change is hard. It doesn't matter how necessary the change, how earnest the investment, or even how deeply we believe. Leading change is often inevitable, but it is difficult for leaders. I could have never imagined how personal it would feel when others resisted the change I was leading. It would have been easy to make unfair judgments about those resisting the change. I fought my tendency to make unfair judgments like, "That teacher is just lazy" or "They clearly don't care as much as the rest of us do."

While these emotional responses might have made me feel better, they were visceral responses and would have kept me from learning how to lead change effectively. Over time, I began to see many understandable reasons why some were resisting change and how we could improve our approach to change while showing intentional respect to those going through it.

Unfortunately, the choice to give up is so much easier than working through the complexity of change. Sometimes, schools settle for an all-out departure from the original goal, but more often, many small concessions throughout change make the final result nearly unrecognizable from the initial vision. Over time, a cyclical "this too shall pass" mentality forms among teachers. They feel that change comes and goes, and they resist when the "tried and true" is quickly abandoned for the new and shiny. When leading change is unsuccessful, little endures, and everyday practice is left vulnerable to the enticement of the next good idea.

You might wonder, "What does change have to do with being a balanced leader?" Admittedly, in my own story, I felt like I had found my footing. I had learned balance from Aaron and then implemented it the hard way on my own. I had come face to face with my own physical limitations, and with the help of loved ones, found well-being in my job. I began to realize who I was as a leader. By all accounts, this chapter comes at what could have been a "happy ending" to my personal leadership story. However, I felt that much more was possible, but it was going to require change and hard work to be the school we knew we could be.

What I woefully underestimated as a young leader was the stress and strain significant change puts on an organization and the individuals within it. As this became clear, it threatened all the strength I had found in myself. It wasn't long before I began second-guessing decisions. In hindsight, I was like the unbalanced leaders I studied, desperately wanting to remove the strain from those I was leading. I found value in coming to my teachers' rescue, and then I started to wonder if I needed to rescue them from me.

There is a reason this chapter on change follows the importance of knowing who you are as a leader. Had it not been for understanding my own strengths and recognizing the skills others could contribute, I am almost certain our school would have abandoned the change process. The loneliness, doubt, and guilt associated with the stress I saw across the campus were all I needed to quit and hide from change altogether. After all I learned, all I had been through, leading change took me right back to the emotional and mental state I felt as a new leader.

Change is difficult. It's complex and stressful for organizations. That said, it can be especially difficult for leaders. Leading change is often confused with micromanaging, not trusting those you lead, or even an attempt to "climb the ladder" to a higher position. As a result, many leaders avoid change. These leaders are often affirmed for this decision. You might have heard someone say something like, "I hire good people and get out of their way." While this is not a bad sentiment, I have seen it used as a platitude leaders hide behind to avoid the challenge of leading necessary change.

Clearly, change should be carefully considered and not taken lightly. However, an organization focused on continuous improvement doesn't have the luxury of hiding from change. If we aspire to be our best as leaders and provide the best experience for those we lead, we must have a plan for how we lead change. It will challenge you as a leader. It will threaten your balance. You may find yourself in places of loneliness and self-doubt. However, if you have a strong foundation—made possible by addressing those elements in the first three chapters of this book—don't allow the complexity of leading change to steal your strength! Change won't ever be easy, but there is a way to lead it efficiently and effectively while staying centered and balanced as a leader. You can be whole while helping your school get better if you approach change the right way.

About Leading Change

Have you ever lifted weights or done a muscle-building exercise? If it has been a while since you exercised or lifted weights, there is nothing quite like the soreness that follows. To grow stronger, we intentionally subject our bodies to damage. As we train, we create micro tears throughout our muscles, triggering inflammation and a response from our body to repair what was damaged. Over time, after many tears and inflammation, the new tissue forms because multiple repairs result in larger, stronger muscles. At a basic physiological level, each of us recognizes that if we want to get stronger, we must subject our body to pain and damage. One day, after many repairs, we are better than we began.

Like a stronger body, most leaders see things in their school they would like to improve. The question we must ask is whether the pain is worth it. Some leaders avoid the pain. Maybe they are intimidated by the legacy of the leader they followed or afraid of making mistakes; keeping the school between the proverbial lines of the lane ahead of them feels challenging enough. Other leaders jump into change like a New Year's exercise commitment. In stark contrast to leaders avoiding change, these leaders come into an organization, upend everything around them, and never recover from the turmoil of the broken school they leave behind. Our goal shouldn't be to find things to change, but we have a responsibility to adjust when necessary to be successful.

Often, as leaders, we are inundated with sales pitches from various companies. The phone rings off the hook, and the email inbox never empties from the promises of what the newest company or resource can do for your students. I would encourage you in the same way I used to encourage my teachers as a principal. I would remind them, "The teacher is the painter; the curriculum is the paint." In other words, if there was ever a curriculum that alone could ensure student learning, there would be no need for teachers. We know that a curriculum is only powerful when, like a master painter with paint, it is blended, mixed, and applied meticulously to achieve the final outcome. Leading change is no different. Change, no matter how needed or valiant, is only as powerful as the craft of those who lead it.

The Lippitt-Knoster Model for Change

When guiding others through change, a well-thought-out plan is just as important as a well-designed lesson for a teacher. To use the muscle-building analogy, you could just go to the gym and start throwing weights around, but the chance of injuring yourself is much higher than finding success. Thankfully, like a detailed exercise plan, there is a great tool for planning your change process. In 1987, Mary Lippitt created a model outlining five critical steps leaders should follow when navigating complex change (Volonte, 2023). In 2000, Tommy Knoster added a sixth step, and the Lippitt-Knoster change model was born (Volonte, 2023). This model provides a step-by-step approach for leading change, along with the foreseeable outcomes should leaders miss steps or not lead change effectively. Figure 4.1 shows the Lippitt-Knoster model.

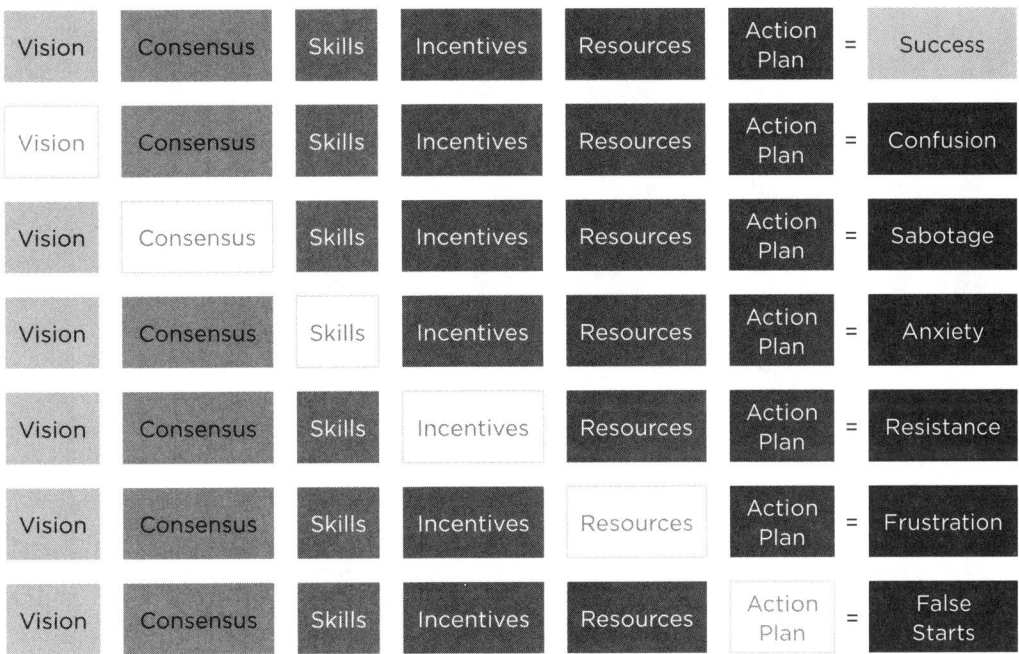

Source: *Adapted from Knoster, Villa, & Thousand, 2000.*

Figure 4.1: Lippitt-Knoster model for managing complex change.

The top of the figure features elements to which leaders must commit to ensure successful change: vision, consensus, skills, incentives, resources, and action plan. As you move down the model, note that missing only one piece from the successful change equation results in a different outcome. It's important to recognize that omitting one of these elements results in unsuccessful change as well as a negative outcome for those you lead. There are six different versions of change failure but only one pathway to success. Any organization that experiences lasting, impactful change will adequately accomplish each of these milestones along the way. However, removing just one of these elements leads to a much different result. Following is a description of each element of this model.

Vision

Without a clear and communicated vision, those we lead will become confused and interpret what they believe is motivating the change. Those in visionless change may blame the change on others or may assume the change is for the personal gain of the leader. If you have ever heard things like, "Well, this is just being forced on us from the central office" or "This is just to pad the principal's résumé," you likely have experienced change without a clear vision. When people don't know the vision for change, they may replace the vision with something that discredits the need for change altogether.

Consensus

If the change process lacks consensus, the organization will likely experience sabotage. If only a single leader or small group believes the change is necessary, others may put forth great effort to alter, stop, or exempt themselves from change. Consensus is reached when two criteria have been met:

1. All points of view have not merely been heard but been actively solicited.

2. The will of the group is evident *even to those who most oppose it*. (DuFour, DuFour, Eaker, Many, Mattos, & Muhammad, 2024, p. 40; italics in original)

This definition requires two steps from leaders. First, ensure the voices of all stakeholders are heard. You can't ignore those who initially don't understand the change or may even oppose it. Doing so does not limit their influence; it simply drives it underground, where sabotage is more likely. However, when the will of the group is evident, it is important to make this clear and not allow a vocal minority to stand in the way. If you have ever been in a school where influential teachers worked to elicit support against a leader or change, there was likely no consensus.

Skills

Teachers who believe in change but don't have the skills to be successful will be anxious. Educators want to feel effective in their jobs. In fact, the higher our level of professional competence, the more likely we are to be engaged and feel connected to our work (BrainFirst Institute, 2024). If we lead a change process without developing the skills needed within others to be successful, it only makes sense that they would experience anxiety and disengagement.

This can happen in schools where veteran staff are asked to make substantial changes in areas where they may be less familiar, such as technology. If you have ever heard people say things like, "I don't even know what she expects us to do" or "I was better when I didn't have to do things the new way," you have likely experienced a change without the needed emphasis on skill development.

Incentives

When people don't see how change could meaningfully improve them or their students, they will resist it. For example, without an understanding of how a specific technological tool might improve my practice or help me reach more students, why would I want to change just for the sake of changing?

We do this so often in schools. New curriculum, new technology, and new expectations are often handed down from a leader. Just because there has been adequate training and the teachers know how to change, it does not mean anyone understands why the change is worth their time and effort. If you've ever heard things like, "Oh great, a new leader and a new curriculum" or "All I have to do is wait out this leader," you have likely experienced the resistance that comes from lack of meaning or incentive in a change.

Resources

If teachers do not have the resources, time, training, or tools to be successful, they will become frustrated. One of the most frustrating things leaders can do is cast a compelling vision, build unifying consensus, and develop teachers toward a change they believe in, only to ignore roadblocks in the way of success.

This often happens with master schedules and budgets in schools. Teachers who believe in the power of collaborative teamwork will be frustrated by a schedule that doesn't allow them to meet. A teacher who is passionate about utilizing engaging technological resources will become frustrated when the only computers their students have access to are so old and slow that they barely function. Making the choice to build such momentum behind change only to allow it to come crashing down because of something structural is unfair and ineffective.

Action Plan

Finally, without a clear plan of action, change will sputter and never take hold. Have you ever found yourself energized during a summer professional development event? Maybe you and a team attended a conference and caught fire with excitement over what is possible for your school. School starts and changes begin to happen, but over time, life happens. Leaders get busy, and teachers focus on other things. The change that only a few months ago brought great excitement and promise is only a memory lost to the rhythm of the day-to-day. These false starts are frustrating for those we lead and compromise change down the line.

While we don't always accomplish what we set out to do, we always end up with the things we settle for (Clear, 2018). Leaders, like a great teacher preparing for instruction, can use the Lippitt-Knoster model to intentionally plan successful change. Begin with a compelling vision and make the effort necessary to build the momentum of consensus for the necessity of the change. Then, ensure that those you lead have the skills needed to engage in change and meaningful incentives to apply the necessary effort. As leaders, when we accomplish these things while also removing barriers, we will see meaningful, lasting change in our schools.

Even the best-planned lesson is not enough to ensure learning for every student, though. The Lippitt-Knoster model provides a strategy for change, but there will be individuals within your organization who require more. No matter how meticulously planned, change causes resistance among those we lead. Viewing those resistant to change similarly to how a teacher sees students struggling to learn, we can assess and support individuals toward success.

Rational and Irrational Resistance to Change

In their book *Time for Change*, Anthony Muhammad and Luis F. Cruz (2019) suggest that resistance to change is predictable and falls into two categories: rational and irrational. Rational resistance to change is logical. Muhammad and Cruz (2019) suggest that someone who doesn't understand the *why* behind the change, doesn't trust those leading the change, or doesn't have the skills or resources to be successful in the change will resist for good reason. As leaders, our responsibility is to meet the needs of each person we lead.

However, there will almost always be people in organizations who, despite being given support and having their needs met, simply don't want to change. This is an irrational resistance to change. They understand and recognize the need for change, have trustworthy leaders of change, and have everything they need to be successful. They simply don't want to change.

Rational Resistance to Change

Most resistance we experience as leaders is rational, meaning there is a logical cause behind the resistance someone is displaying. If there is a logical cause, this suggests there is a logical solution as well. Not long ago, I had the opportunity to speak to new school leaders. The day ended with some words from a highly regarded, long-tenured superintendent from a school district nearby. As he stood in front of us, he promised to share the wisdom he had gained from several years in school leadership. I found myself leaning forward in my chair, pen and paper ready, eager to learn from someone so experienced. Within moments, not only was my pen and notepad back in my backpack, but it also took all I had to even stay in the room.

With great pride and a sly grin, this decorated superintendent boasted about the number of teachers and principals he "ran off" in his tenure. He thought his greatest attribute and reason for success was his ability to spot and clear anyone out of his path that couldn't meet his standards. Appalled by how flippantly and disrespectfully he spoke about educators in his district, I looked around the room, expecting to catch the shocked gazes of people just like me. Sadly, I saw a room full of young leaders nodding their heads and hanging on to his every word.

Over the years, I have unfortunately seen this kind of behavior in leaders all too often. Are high standards important among leaders? Of course they are. To be clear, I have had people leave an organization I led because they were unwilling to be part of the change process to which we collectively committed. I have also had the misfortune of having to play a major role in the exit of some because of their ineffectiveness or unwillingness to commit to professional expectations. These were incredibly difficult experiences. There should be nothing within a leader that takes pride in the removal of professional educators.

Instead, great leaders are willing, only when they have no other choice, to do difficult things on behalf of the responsibility they have to their students, staff, and community. Leaders who champion the removal of teachers like the conquering of an enemy often do so as a weak attempt to feign credibility they'll likely never find among those they lead. What they treat like "notches in their belt" are often seen as holes in their credibility. Great leaders multiply others toward sustainable greatness (Wiseman, 2017). They recognize that, like a teacher leading students through learning something new and challenging, it is the responsibility of the leader to teach, differentiate, support, and do everything possible to ensure the success of those they lead.

The Causes of Rational Resistance

Remember the beginning of your educational career? I vividly remember an observation from my mentor during my first year in the classroom. I came to school that day in a freshly pressed shirt and tie, which was a big deal for a twenty-two-year-old. I also remember the hours in which I had painstakingly prepared the most perfect lesson plan for my observer—three pages, color-coded and laminated. I proudly handed over the lesson plan before welcoming students to the room. Within the first minute, a student got sick coming into the classroom. Another student slipped and fell in the mess and began crying. I frantically tried to escort both the sick student and the student who was now covered in the unspeakable mess to the office while directing the incoming student traffic around the mess.

When I got back, students were just randomly standing around the room talking and laughing about what had just occurred. Nearly seven minutes later, I was almost fifteen minutes into a forty-minute class period and nowhere near what was envisioned in the three color-coded pages worth of planning. Determined to rush through the plans I had spent so much time on, I pushed students through the lesson with little regard whatsoever to whether anyone learned a thing. Student engagement was awful, their output was pitiful, and the day was wasted, not by what I couldn't control, but by my determination to be so focused on what I was teaching that I didn't care if anyone learned. Every component of the lesson plan was met in what would go down as one of my all-time worst displays of teaching.

Have you ever experienced a leader who took this approach? Committed to a new initiative, they rush their staff through checkpoints on their planned path to change. Along the way, no one is learning, and very little is improving, but the leader, so singularly focused on checking off their "change to-do list," is shocked when things don't go to plan. Leading change is like teaching a classroom. What you teach matters much less than what others learn. Like a master teacher, transformational leaders constantly adjust their approach to fulfill the needs of their learners.

As noted previously, predictability is essential throughout the change process. Muhammad and Cruz (2019) write that a leader has the responsibility to ensure everyone who is engaging in change understands *why* the change is worth their effort, that they have people within the organization they trust to guide them through change, and that they have been given the training and resources needed to be successful. If these needs are not met, people will resist change for good reason, and the leader is to blame (Muhammad & Cruz, 2019). These three needs align with the Lippitt-Knoster model in helping us to preplan the needs of our entire organization.

Even with a great plan, change affects individual teachers. Great instruction, like a well-planned change, will work for most students, but some individuals will need focused support. To reach these students, a classroom teacher must diagnose misconceptions, assess student learning, and support them where they are in their learning. Leading change is no different.

The SCARF Model

Regardless of how well you plan, you will still experience resistance to change. Your ability to understand this resistance helps support those you lead. David Rock (2008) is known for his SCARF model, which states that our perception and behavior toward change are dramatically impacted by the impact the change has on our **S**tatus, **C**ertainty, **A**utonomy, **R**elatedness, and **F**airness. His model suggests that people function predictably in social situations and identifies a brain-based approach for how to collaborate and influence others (Rock, 2008).

In our book *The Foundation for Change* (Vander Els & Ray, 2024), Jonathan G. Vander Els and I dig deep into these five areas as a blueprint for creating collective commitments in schools. For the sake of this chapter, however, we can use these five areas to predict, diagnose, and adjust our approach to resistance among those we lead.

Status

Status is our sense of importance or prestige and our perception of how we are seen by others (Rock, 2008). People will predictably resist change that threatens their professional status. Some common status threats are a change to how a teacher is perceived among their peers, how they are perceived in the outside community, or how their performance could be impacted by change.

When I think about threats to status, I think about Stacy, one of the teachers working at my school when I implemented the new policy that parents could no longer choose their child's teacher. She was recognized throughout our building and community as a great teacher. However, she resisted our new policy because it threatened the status she had spent many years building.

Initially, Stacy's resistance caused me to form an unfair opinion of her. I assumed she was uncommitted and selfish. The truth was, she had simply learned how to succeed in the toxic system she worked in. Over many conversations, I learned that Stacy cared deeply about being a great teacher, not just for her status but for her students. With a clearer understanding and empathy for her position, I was able to work alongside her to build a better school where she became one of the greatest champions of necessary change.

Certainty

Certainty is the stability we crave that provides security in our profession (Rock, 2008). Behind our need for certainty is the fear of uncertainty. Someone's fear of uncertainty does not necessarily mean they are unwilling to change. Confidence is often rooted in results. Threats to certainty impacted the elementary school where I was principal. Many teachers had instructional units that students, families, and our community had come to love. These units were fun and engaging, but they didn't meet the expectations we held for rigor and learning. Teachers resisted changing these units because of the positive feedback they received year after year for their work.

Autonomy

Autonomy is the feeling of control or choice in our professional lives (Rock, 2008). Every person we lead through change likely has previous experiences with change. Like certainty, autonomy represents what experience has shown teachers what works best for them. Over time, teachers—especially veteran teachers—experience a great deal of change. Every time teachers feel change removes their professional autonomy only to leave them with something less effective, they will be that much more likely to hold tightly to autonomy in the future.

The threat to autonomy was a challenge in the high school where I was principal. Data in our school suggested some teachers were struggling to reach students the way their peers did. When it came time to examine teaching practices and adjust instructional techniques, some teachers quickly blamed students instead of their practices. For them, change felt embarrassing and frightening, and it was easier to blame students than risk changing and failing.

Relatedness

Relatedness is the feeling of connection we share with others (Rock, 2008). Most of us have what we might consider our "work family." Relatedness with these people is always important; but for some, lifelong, personal friendships may have begun by teaching together. Leaders need to be mindful of change that might cause divisions in these relationships. I have experienced this, especially when distributing leadership.

One deeply respected high school teacher was hesitant to engage in a change they believed in because it might isolate them from those who didn't want to change. In the elementary school I served, there was a pair of teachers who had become like sisters over their years of working together. When we needed to change their teaching assignments, the resistance felt personal. For them, it was like breaking up a friendship rather than teaching new content. Unfortunately, we couldn't avoid changing the teaching assignments. However, when we asked them to co-lead a new school club, we gave them the chance to work together again. This joint venture couldn't replace teaching together, but it helped ensure they had the chance to work alongside one another.

Fairness

Finally, fairness is the belief that the results of change are just and equitable (Rock, 2008). Not all change impacts everyone in the organization the same way. This happens in schools all the time. Often, change dramatically impacts core content teachers, while extracurricular teachers are exempt. Even as a former band director, I was guilty of this as a leader. There were times when my hyperfocus on core content teachers was unfair. There were also times when my misguided attempt to be fair meant I was asking some teachers to do things that didn't make sense at all. In both instances, I felt resistance because the change was not fair for all involved.

As you read through the five SCARF components, individuals you lead may have come to mind. These five areas are triggers for rational resistance among people in any organization. If you notice resistance in your organization in one of these five areas, those resisting aren't bad people. They are human beings! These five areas provide blueprints for approaching change while understanding and humanizing rational resistance. From there, like a master teacher, we can adjust our practices to ensure growth for everyone.

Appropriate Response to Rational Resistance to Change

In the preceding pages, we have considered change from the perspective of the organization, school, and individuals. All approaches share one thing in common: they position leaders in a rightful place of responsibility for the outcomes of those they lead. Leaders can respectfully work to understand and address the concerns of those they lead. This doesn't necessarily make change easier, but respectfully navigating the concerns of those we lead displays empathy, care, and respect throughout the school. By understanding the sources of resistance, leaders can support those they lead and reduce the emotional responses of people frightened and isolated amid change.

Regardless of how well a team of leaders addresses the *why*, *who*, and *how* of change, a school will not move forward without an established culture of accountability (Collins, 2001). There will be those whose concerns (refer to The SCARF Model on pages 77–79) you support but who still simply do not want to change. In this situation, a school is only as successful as the worst adult behavior its leaders are willing to accept.

As leaders, we can't forget that we promote what we permit. The success of our work and the measure of our credibility can all unravel by choosing to ignore irrational resistance. Leaders who want to see their school implement and sustain meaningful change must have a plan for how they will structure accountability.

Irrational Resistance to Change

Although most resistance is rational, Muhammad and Cruz (2019) remind us that some resistance is irrational. This occurs when someone understands the *why*, has a trusting *who*, and has all the *what* they need to successfully implement change. In these rare cases, leaders must clarify that they are not suggesting people participate in the collective work of change; they expect it (Muhammad & Cruz, 2019). While this is never easy, a leader who avoids this confrontation diminishes the hard work of every other person in the school.

Ultimately, all leaders will make some of the people they lead uncomfortable. Effective leaders make ineffective teachers uncomfortable. Ineffective leaders make effective teachers uncomfortable. When your school embarks on a change process the way this chapter describes, these conversations are much less confrontational than they are protective. Addressing irrational resistance is the responsibility of leaders who are unwilling to allow the momentum built throughout their entire school to be threatened by someone who simply won't do what everyone else has committed to do together.

Now, stop and reflect on how rational or irrational resistance affects change at your school. Record your thoughts in a notebook or journal.

> **Stop and Reflect: Does Resistance to Change Create Isolation on Your Campus? How Is Fear Feeding Resistance in Your School?**
>
> Have you been through a messy change process? What did resistance feel like, and how did it impact those in the school? Take a moment to reflect on the emotions, fear, and anxiety you experienced in those who resisted change.
>
> Now, is resistance to change present on your campus? Is it emotionally charged and hurtful, or is it understandable and relatable? Take a moment to journal your experience as someone in an organization or leading an organization through change.
>
> Record your thoughts before you continue reading.

A Structure for Healthy School Accountability

A clear process of accountability works very similar to a tiered pyramid of interventions in a Response to Intervention (RTI) at Work™ structure (Mattos, Buffum, Malone, Cruz, Dimich, & Schuhl, 2025). The inverted pyramid of interventions, outlined in *Taking Action* (Mattos et al., 2025), is intended to progressively provide layers of support to ensure each student reaches grade-level proficiency. These layers of support are divided into three separate tiers.

- **Tier 1:** Tier 1, initial grade-level core instruction, is universal in its focus on ensuring every student learns the most essential skills in their current grade or course.

- **Tier 2:** Tier 2 instruction is the extra time and support teachers provide to ensure students learn grade-level skills. The premise of Tier 2 support is that no matter how effective the initial instruction is, some students will need extra support to ensure learning.

- **Tier 3:** Tier 3 instruction is the intensive reinforcements and support provided to students who enter the school year more than two years behind in a key skill. While the teacher will undoubtedly do their best to meet the needs of students missing critical skills, they will most likely need targeted instruction in their area of deficiency to help close the critical learning gaps they are experiencing.

One of the fundamental components of this tiered system is that students get every level of support they need to learn. In other words, a student who has substantial gaps in their learning and needs Tier 3 intervention and reinforcement should not get them at the cost of Tier 2 reteaching of grade-level curriculum or the critical initial instruction of Tier 1.

I encourage you to think about professional accountability in a similar tiered fashion. In Tier 1, the expectations for change are presented to staff as universal, relevant, and clear. However, like the struggle students experience while learning new skills, embodying change doesn't happen the same way for every professional. If we approach change the same way we approach student learning, Tier 2 offers support for staff and colleagues as we each engage in the transformation together. The great thing about this level of support is that no positional authority is required. It can come from a partner teacher, a friend, or a teacher leader. Finally, like Tier 3 supports for students individually struggling, we must recognize that some individuals will need more support than others during the change process. This could consist of one-on-one coaching, scheduled check-ins, or any other targeted support to help an individual who is falling behind in the change process.

Approaching accountability through the lens of a multitiered system of supports keeps the focus on changes in behaviors. The RTI structure is intended to ensure learning. In the same way, a tiered accountability system for change focuses less on the implementation of a new initiative and much more on the individuals and how they embody change throughout the organization.

Tier 1 Accountability

In RTI, Tier 1 is the initial, grade-level core instruction to which every student has access. This is no different for the change process. Expectations for adult behaviors should be guaranteed and viable. When a school has an established purpose (mission), a common focus unites the entire organization (Vander Els & Ray, 2024).

However, simply having a school mission statement does not ensure the change in behaviors that occur in meaningful change. To do this, schools must be clear and practical in establishing collective commitments. Vander Els and I explain, "While your mission states your fundamental purpose, your collective commitments are the daily changes in adult behaviors you practice to live out the mission" (Vander Els & Ray, 2024, p. 76). The more universally clear and concise the expectations for behavior, the easier accountability becomes (Luntz, 2007).

Collective commitments translate the *why* and *what* of change (Muhammad & Cruz, 2019) into easily observable new behaviors. In this way, collective commitments, or the Tier 1 of a tiered system of accountability, function similarly to learning proficiency in the classroom. A teacher team delivering quality Tier 1 instruction will measure effectiveness not in their delivery of the curriculum or lesson, but in student learning. This is why clear collective commitments, which explicitly describe new behaviors, are so critical to a tiered system of accountability. If staff don't understand exactly what it means to embody change, it is unfair to hold them accountable. However, when you describe the behaviors you are working toward, especially in comparison to behaviors you currently practice, you have a guaranteed and viable expectation for all.

The clearer and more explicit these new behaviors, the fairer and more effective this behavioral shift will be. It is also much easier to hold each other accountable because we are adjusting clearly defined behaviors, not measuring intentions or feelings. We wouldn't test students on something they were never taught. Similarly, it's not fair to hold people accountable for something that has not been explicitly defined throughout the school.

Tier 2 Accountability

The second tier of professional accountability is acknowledgment and support. If your mission for change is clear, and you have defined universal behaviors that help you reach the compelling future you aspire to, teachers throughout the building can provide supportive accountability. Since they do not have positional authority, they do not have the ability to formally hold others accountable (Muhammad & Cruz, 2019). Instead, they can provide support without condemnation. This could be something as simple as checking in or offering to help someone who is falling behind.

The impact of this conversation is twofold. First, the change process belongs to more than just the principal; it is part of the whole school. Second, the foundation for a strong school culture is being built through collaborative peer support. This establishes the trusting *who* Muhammad and Cruz (2019) say is critically important for those experiencing change throughout the building. Just as important, if a principal is going to ask members of a distributed leadership team to take this step, the principal should communicate this expectation to the entire staff. The staff should understand their collective commitments (Tier 1) and that the principal is asking everyone to support one another in embodying these new behaviors (Tier 2). This makes peer accountability much easier because everyone understands the commitment to change across the school.

Tier 3 Accountability

Sometimes, expectations are clearly established, and staff have provided supportive accountability, but an individual still may not have adjusted their behaviors to meet the school's expectations. At this point, only the person in positional authority can provide Tier 3 accountability (Muhammad & Cruz, 2019). Like the expectation of the entire staff to provide supportive accountability (Tier 2), this process should be clearly articulated to the entire school. However, just because the person in positional authority is providing direct support, this doesn't necessarily mean it is time to move to disciplinary action for someone needing individualized accountability.

The first goal should always be to provide support in bringing behaviors in line with expectations. In this situation, accountability for the behavior now belongs to the positional leader. The principal assumes the role of "culture keeper"—the line in the sand on the most important expectations. The leader also commits to following up to ensure the individual's behavior begins to shift. When a leader follows through in their responsibility to actively address behaviors, it makes it easier for staff to provide supportive accountability to one another throughout the change process.

Strategies to Diagnose, Understand, and Address Resistance to Change

In a school with a multitiered system of supports for students, the tiers are only as effective as the school's ability to meet the needs of each student. The quality of a tiered system of professional accountability is dependent on its ability to identify and support the specific needs of each individual. If resistance to change were somehow predictable, we could develop a plan for addressing it. Like a team of teachers meeting the needs of all students, a school can differentiate the approach to change and remove some of the struggle and emotion often associated with resistance. The following are strategies for diagnosing, understanding, and addressing resistance to change in your building.

Use the SCARF Model for Individuals

Rock (2008) created the SCARF model to show the universal areas in which change often impacts individuals. His assertion is that each of us will respond negatively to any change that we feel threatens our status, certainty, autonomy, relatedness, or fairness. Rock's (2008) model allows us to seek understanding of the underlying concerns that bring about resistant behaviors of individuals in a school.

With this in mind, the SCARF model provides an approach for diagnosing and supporting individuals who have relatable struggles with change (Rock, 2008). Figure 4.2 offers a tool you could use to assess resistance and support individuals within your organization. Like a teacher assessing students in the classroom, leaders can use this tool as a preassessment to help predict resistance before it occurs. Before ever committing to change, a leader could use the second column to anticipate how the SCARF of those directly impacted by change could be threatened.

SCARF Component	Possible Ways This SCARF Component Could Be Threatened	Fears or Assumptions Linked to This SCARF Component	Ways to Ease the Threat	Ways to Support This SCARF Component
Status				
Certainty				
Autonomy				
Relatedness				
Fairness				

Source: Adapted from Rock, 2008.

Figure 4.2: SCARF individual resistance assessment tool.

*Visit **go.SolutionTree.com/educatorwellness** for a free reproducible version of this figure.*

Still, it is almost impossible to proactively plan for all resistance to change. A leader could use this tool to empathize with an individual resisting change. While a leader can use the "preassessment" approach to consider how the SCARF of their entire organization could be threatened, approaching this with an individual in mind is more specific and tailored. With care and empathy, the leader can then plan ways to support an individual resisting change. The following explains how to complete each column in the assessment tool.

Possible Ways This SCARF Component Could Be Threatened

In the second column, list the ways change could threaten individuals or groups in each of the five SCARF components. If you are using the tool to preassess or predict resistance, I suggest starting with how change could cause resistance throughout the entire school or within large groups. Like a teacher who plans instruction for class and then reteaches individuals by need, plan for large-scale implementation and then respond when you experience individual issues. If you are using the tool to seek understanding about what could be causing an individual to resist, then the second column should focus solely on the behaviors or experiences of the individual.

Fears or Assumptions Linked to This SCARF Component

In the third column, take a moment to consider how a threat to this SCARF component could morph into a gripping, fearful assumption. When we feel change threatens one of these five areas, emotions can rapidly turn discomfort into real professional fear. For example, if your school is shifting to a collaborative culture in which teachers openly share the results from their classroom assessments, teachers' status likely could be threatened. Such status threats could be very frightening for those experiencing them. By putting yourself in their shoes, you can imagine how fear could throw gasoline on the fire of any threat.

Imagine the inner dialogue for a veteran teacher who might worry that sharing her data with others could expose her as a less-skilled teacher than others perceive her. Now one of her former students is a new teacher on the team. What if her data were worse than her former student's? How embarrassing! Several years ago, she had a difficult class, and her principal at the time embarrassed her in front of her colleagues when he compared her classroom to a zoo. That was the hardest year of her career. Her most recent principal saw her skill set and gave her the chance to lead professional development for the staff several times. How could she, the person who was teaching her peers, run the risk of having the lowest data on the team? No one would respect her anymore. She likely would never get to lead professional development again. She goes home, can't sleep, and rehashes the pain and embarrassment she felt all those years ago. She knows she can't go through that again. Maybe she just needs to find a new job.

The leader in this scenario sees sharing data as a chance for teachers to learn together and help one another reach all students. When this teacher resists change, she is unlikely to reveal the trauma of her past professional embarrassment to her new leader. Often, instead of being further embarrassed, adults, just like students in the classroom, use behavior to shield themselves from the vulnerability of weakness or fear. For the leader, sharing data seems logical and is clearly best practice. Without taking a moment to seek to understand the perspective of this teacher, the leader could quickly become frustrated and make rash judgments about her quality as a teacher or her professionalism, when all along, her resistance is completely understandable.

Ways to Ease the Threat

With renewed empathy toward the person resisting change, the next step is to write down some systematic ways you could ease or calm this threat, either before change occurs or when someone resists change. The goal of this column is not to "fix" the resistance of groups or individuals. Instead, it is to remove the power from emotions or fear associated with the SCARF element being threatened. Whether predicting resistance before change or responding to resistance during change, easing the threat to SCARF will likely happen on a large scale for the organization.

Even in the case of diagnosing resistance for a single individual, that person is likely not the only one who feels threat or concern in this area. A savvy leader who anticipates threat to status through change may gather veteran teachers for input on how to share data without condemnation or ranking of professional effectiveness. If their goal is to build a safe culture for professional vulnerability, validating their experiences invites teachers to express similar concerns and contribute to a solution.

Ways to Support This SCARF Component

The last component of the tool is planning support for those who resist. In the example of the teacher who is afraid of losing her status, a leader could suggest she leads an upcoming professional learning session. Perhaps the leader could display vulnerability by asking her to help contribute to improving the leader's professional practice. There are endless possibilities, and we might not find a strategy that immediately resolves the fear behind the resistance. Still, consider the focus of this approach to resistance by going through this simple process. Just like a teacher reteaching individual students, it may take a few different approaches or techniques before something works, but empathetically working to diagnose resistance is much more targeted and effective.

A simple tool like this allows a leader or leadership team to predict resistance as well as diagnose it when it occurs. With an individual in mind, a leader could seek to understand the fear behind the resistance and where the fear could originate. Then, leaders have specific ways they can respectfully support and protect those resisting the change. Like a common assessment for a teacher team, this could provide the information needed to show areas for targeted growth throughout the building.

Further, this tool allows you to objectively gather information and ideas while cutting through emotion and judgment. While it's helpful for leaders, it's even more powerful when shared with a leadership team. Sharing strategies to ease individual fears builds empathy throughout a school. Alongside a principal willing to address areas of need, this approach to shared leadership can shift a school culture methodically and effectively.

Use the Lippitt-Knoster Model to Support Teams and Systems

While SCARF helps you assess and meet the needs of individuals resisting change, the Lippitt-Knoster model provides a playbook for assessing and supporting teams or schools going through change. (Refer to page 71 for more information about the Lippitt-Knoster model.) It addresses negative symptoms of resistance, such as confusion, sabotage, anxiety, resistance, frustration, and false starts. These are real, relatable symptoms present in a school that is missing key components to a successful change process.

Figure 4.3 (page 88) provides a holistic means of assessing the effectiveness of the change process across a school. If SCARF is like addressing learning by student and need, the Lippitt-Knoster model is akin to finding trends in building data. The leadership team can use this tool to consider the overall trends in their organization specific to the change process, including the negative symptoms of unmet needs, steps it has taken to support this need, new strategies to support this need, and the best people to meet this need. Rather than focusing on any single individual, this tool helps make broader changes to support the organization as a whole. Then, the team can use this information to plan new ways to support this need utilizing those who are most likely to be successful.

When leaders notice negative symptoms throughout their team or school, they can use this model to pinpoint areas where they could focus efforts to improve the change process. By focusing on one of the negative symptoms of the Lippitt-Knoster model, leaders can consider what they have done to support this need in their school, reflect on what has had the most positive impact in this area, and then plan new ways to further secure a particular need for staff.

Negative Symptom of Resistance	How have we supported this need in the past?	Is there a new need that requires targeted support?	How could we support this need in new ways?	Who are the best people in our school to provide this support?
Confusion (Lack of Vision)				
Sabotage (Lack of Consensus)				
Anxiety (Lack of Skills)				
Resistance (Lack of Incentives)				
Frustration (Lack of Resources)				
False Starts (Lack of Action Plan)				

Source: Adapted from Lippitt-Knoster, Villa, & Thousand, 2000.

Figure 4.3: Lippitt-Knoster systemic resistance assessment tool.

*Visit **go.SolutionTree.com/educatorwellness** for a free reproducible version of this figure.*

For example, when a leader begins to recognize anxiety throughout a team or school, they can use this model to remind them this could be symptomatic of a lack of skills among those going through change. Through reflection, the leader may remember the training they went through together and what seemed to make most sense to teachers. However, if teachers are expressing anxiety about a particular part of the change, this would be a perfect place for specific, targeted training to build confidence and competence among the staff. Diagnostically assessing negative symptoms of change and providing intentional support protects the change while also validating the experiences of those going through it.

A highly effective teacher team uses assessment to identify the needs of their students, not necessarily to test or assign grades. With clarity, they can support student learning by name and need. Great schools and leaders treat resistance the same way. The SCARF model and the Lippitt-Knoster model provide assessment tools to better understand the source of resistance within either individuals or your school. So, a great leader functions like an interventionist. With empathy, support, and understanding, a leader has the information they need to strengthen change and those experiencing it. Remember, most resistance is rational and understandable. As such, most responses from leaders should be with understanding, learning, and support.

Conclusion

If you have never personally felt the isolation of leading change, there are few greater stressors. Change is messy because people are messy. However, approaching change rationally and strategically removes emotion, improves clarity, and provides a path toward success. With a system of supports and accountability, leaders can share the load that all too often falls on a single set of shoulders otherwise. A clear plan that lowers stress and shares the burden is a recipe for sustainable, balanced leadership.

Ultimately, every leader will have to navigate resistance and professional anxiety. The leaders who seek to understand the perspective of those they lead and intentionally adjust their approach to meet their needs show respect and care and have a much greater chance for success. Change is never easy, but it can be successful.

CHAPTER 5

Sharing Leadership

It was unquestionably the high point of my career. Only a few short years since I started as a new principal and felt the weight of my own self-doubt threatening to crush me, our campus was recognized as a Model PLC and received nearly $150,000 in state reward funding for our exemplary performance and growth. Our school was no longer a B campus; we were one of the very best elementary schools in our entire state. We had not just survived change, but because of the collective effort of an incredible group of professionals, we were thriving.

At the same time, Aaron was named the new high school principal in our district. With a hero's welcome, he addressed the staff and students at the close of the year in preparation for his ascent to the role of principal. A few weeks later, on a hot, sticky June evening in Arkansas, Aaron and I left our school board meeting and drove together to see his new office. Like a kindergartener at show and tell, he pointed out every inch of the office, meticulously planned to represent the man who wanted nothing more from his career than to assume this very seat.

My sons and I drove him home that evening without a single care in the world. Summer was upon us, my best buddy was the town hero, and somewhere amid it all, I had managed to find myself as a leader. It was the week of Father's Day, and Aaron was taking his teenage son, Landry, to see a Texas Rangers game. Despite his insistence that he could make it work, I convinced him to forego our weekly ritual of Saturday breakfast to ensure they would have plenty of time to make it to the baseball game. The next day, only hours after I dropped him off at his house, on their way to the game together, an oncoming car crossed the middle line and hit their car head-on. Aaron and Landry were gone.

The next couple of weeks were a blur. Aaron's shared funeral with Landry was too big to house at any church in our community. Instead, crammed into our high school basketball arena, thousands of people paid their respects to two of the greatest men I had ever known. Amid my personal grief, our district tasked me with the incredible honor and responsibility of assuming the position destined for my best friend.

With many leadership lessons learned and a desire to honor a friend I revered, it would seem natural that I would employ the things I had learned in my experience to this point. Instead, I found myself reverting to the basest sense of who I was. Crippled by an inability to fill the shoes of my best friend and hero, I was like a brand-new leader all over again, constantly overthinking and overcompensating. It took an excruciatingly ineffective first semester to help me grapple with the reality I was trying to avoid: I was not enough to fill the void my best buddy left. I needed help, and I needed it fast.

Outside of this painful reality, I may have never found myself surrounded by the team of people who would ultimately right the ship for our high school. It was the start of the spring semester of the 2021–2022 school year, and a room full of teachers, instructional coaches, and leaders joined me and meticulously dissected the challenges of our postpandemic reality. Honestly, the meeting was painful. It was clear that on the heels of the pandemic and great loss, our school was a ship without an anchor. As the leader, that began with me. It was time to decide who we were and confront the mess of our current reality.

Students weren't coming to school. There were major gaps in learning. Student behavior was challenging beyond anything the school had seen. Our master schedule didn't meet our needs. Our expectations for students were not unified. We hadn't established what mattered most. We were a shell of who we wanted to be. Once we ripped off the Band-Aid and laid bare the gnarled truth in black and white, the response was not defeat or disgust. Instead, there was purpose, resolution, and results.

We went item by item, like a shopping list, with intentional ways to improve. We restructured the roles and procedures of our office staff, prioritized what our students needed to learn, clarified our behavioral procedures and changed our policies, made a substantial change to our master schedule, and defined success for our students. Not one of these changes came from a "great idea" or a desire to innovate. They were all a response to the clarity only achieved when we recognized the difference between our desired state and our current reality.

What felt like a campus enduring a struggling new leader in year one became a 25 percent increase in student attendance, a redefinition of school culture, a universal increase in student achievement, and a revitalized school only twelve months later. Even though I had personally benefitted from shared leadership on my elementary campus, in my most vulnerable state as a leader, I once again reverted to the crippling weight of trying to be enough on my own. Thankfully, once again, a united team of shared leaders radically changed our campus for the better.

Over the last four chapters, we have walked a specific path together. The path is laid out through my personal story as well as many stories I have heard from educational leaders around the world. To be your very best, begin with you. Your job should not cost you what matters most. Time and again, I've seen highly educated, decorated leaders who somehow found a way to deny themselves the most basic elements of what they physically need to survive. Wellness is not a luxury. It is a prerequisite to you being your best for those you lead. When we know ourselves and intentionally design our roles to highlight our strengths, we are more effective and fulfilled and have the chance to find the strength in others. This is important because even if we wish we could avoid it, growing pains are part of the change necessary for continuous improvement. Now, with a foundation of strength built in you the person and you the leader, it is time to acknowledge the last fundamental truth of this book: *You are not enough*.

Those four words may cause you a little discomfort. As leaders, we like to think we can swoop in like superheroes and single-handedly lead our organizations to greatness. The sooner we recognize this is not only impossible but a completely unfair expectation, the sooner we will feel the freedom of sharing leadership. As I was writing this book, I couldn't help but wonder why this is hard for so many leaders. In reflection, I think the answer is simple. If we live our professional lives out of balance, feeling physically depleted, putting out fires, and avoiding change, we have built several layers of unsustainable individualism into our roles. This book is meant to help you be your most effective, efficient, and whole. When we approach leadership as a shared endeavor, then leading with balance, well-being, joy, and continuous improvement seems much less daunting.

About Sharing Leadership

Your job is complex and requires a great deal from you as an individual. Hopefully, you have also felt validated and empowered to find the balance of efficiency and wellness that will make you the best leader for your school or district. That said, the point of this last chapter is to make the case that regardless of your talents, focus, balance, or well-being, leadership is too big for you. Leadership is a team sport. It might seem strange that I would have to write a chapter to admonish you to share the massive weight of your job with the most capable around you. That said, just like me, so many leaders place unrealistic pressure on themselves to "have all the answers" instead of sharing the load.

John Eades (2021), CEO of LearnLoft, a company focused on helping leaders, said it best: "Having had the opportunity to teach and coach thousands of leaders, the most common cause of not sharing insight with others or becoming a thought leader isn't selfishness; it's often imposter syndrome." Just like protecting our balance or prioritizing our health, sharing leadership doesn't make us weaker; it makes the school and those we lead better. We must get out of our own way, though.

A Definition of Shared Leadership

Shared leadership is a recipe for greater team effectiveness. However, simply forming a team is not the same as sharing leadership. In 2014, Danni Wang, David A. Waldman, and Zhen Zhang conducted a meta-analysis about the impact of shared leadership. They found that not all approaches to shared leadership are effective. Across the many forms of leadership, transformational leaders, those who inspire followers to transcend their own self-interests for the good of the organization, have the most impact (Bass & Riggio, 2006). When compared to a team collaboratively working toward this type of leadership, those who simply created a team to delegate tasks were substantially less successful (Wang et al., 2014). The work of your team is equally as important as who is on it.

The power of shared leadership lies less in "more hands" than it does in "more perspectives." This suggests a shared leadership team should be working toward the more complex things throughout the school that most benefit from the collective genius only a team can bring (Wang et al., 2014). Among these, few have the power of leveraged relationships, the adjustment of your school culture, or a focus on your major goals (Fernandez & Velasquez, 2023). I remember many times as a new leader wondering why anyone I led would trust or follow me. However, when leadership is shared, we gain the influence and credibility of those on our team.

Shared leadership may be most valuable when collectively establishing school culture. School culture encompasses the shared beliefs, values, norms, and behaviors of the individuals within a school community. It is the "personality" of the school, shaping the way teachers interact with students, how students interact with each other, and the overall climate of the school (Muhammad, 2018). In *The Foundation for Change* (Vander Els & Ray, 2024), Vander Els and I discuss the importance of a shared leadership team establishing the behaviors necessary to adjust school culture over time. We state that one of the major roles of shared leadership is determining the type of school you want to become and which behaviors to adjust to embody this. Each school and district have distinct personalities. Through the influence and relationships of a shared leadership team, a school can move from its current state to the school it hopes to become.

Finally, shared leadership sets and leads the school toward meaningful goals. Goals are the measurable steps between your current reality and the school you hope to become (Vander Els & Ray, 2024). When done well, they are motivating and purposeful. Great schools have large, organizational goals as well as smaller goals that drive individuals and teams throughout the building. Shared leadership brings influence to accomplishing goals, but it also brings perspective to the segments of the school they represent.

A school counselor may have a completely different interpretation of and motivation from a goal than a science teacher. This is not only OK; it is one of the great strengths of shared leadership. Without multiple perspectives, goals are only as meaningful as a single leader's ability to incentivize them to every member of the school. However, when a goal is created and owned by a diverse team of leaders, there is personalization and unification through common focus.

Leader Isolation

In the previous chapter, I mentioned the isolation of leadership. When the proverbial "buck" stops with us, there is pressure that few others understand. Leaders are faced with no-win situations and challenging circumstances. Leaders are also often somewhat separated from those they work with. Once we become "the boss," even longstanding professional relationships we've had for years change. Add the never-ending onslaught of tasks that compete for our attention, and it is easy to see how we begin to feel like an outsider in our own school. In many ways, this is difficult to avoid. However, leaders often do things that needlessly add to the isolating nature of our positions instead of connecting us to those we lead.

Even in schools working to build a collaborative working environment for teachers, leaders often allow themselves to be the exception. If we believe that no single teacher can meet the needs of a class full of students, why would we expect leaders to meet the needs of an entire school? Sometimes, this isolated approach is self-imposed, while other times it is learned. When leaders find themselves in a place of self-isolation, it usually begins with a lack of clarity and confidence.

Sadly, many of us entered our role as leaders without really understanding what success looked like. As a result, as discussed earlier, we easily equate being busy, making herculean efforts, or solving every problem with success. Can you imagine if we did this to our students? "Okay, kids, we're not going to tell you what we expect, but everyone is watching, and you will get a grade by how well you perform. Good luck!" It's laughable, but it is also what many leaders experience.

In these scenarios, leaders often fill their time to the point that they have no chance for connection, or they retreat from the inevitable negative feedback that occurs in difficult scenarios. Instead, leaders need the clarity discussed in chapter 3 (page 51). What are your strengths, focuses, and best ways to use your time? You shouldn't settle for isolated leadership, but if you are not purposeful in your focus and connections, it may be the outcome you never intended.

Other leaders learn isolation from their leaders or system. Many habits are inherited. When they don't know what to do, they look for people who do. Others' example becomes the foundation their own experiences build from. As a result, leaders likely do things professionally that they have never stopped to consider the reason behind (Duhigg, 2012). Those we lead learn our "professional currency"—especially those who aspire to lead themselves.

Think back to when you first became a teacher; there were probably things you did only because a teacher you knew or respected did them, too. A principal who sees their superintendent never include others in making decisions is more likely to do the same thing themselves. Maybe they feel this is the expectation of the superintendent, or maybe it is subconscious. Teacher leaders who experience a principal who never seeks their input on important decisions are less likely to go to others when they face challenging situations themselves. Leader isolation can be contagious.

A New Definition of Leadership

Before you can set the stage for shared leadership in your school, you need a clear definition of what it means to be a leader. Muhammad and Cruz (2019) define *leadership* this way: "Leadership is not a position; it is a set of actions that positively shape the climate and culture of the working environment" (p. 2). When you consider your school, who has the most influence on those they work with? These are people who others trust and who oftentimes hold a great deal more influence than those in positional authority (Muhammad & Cruz, 2019). If there are people in your school who influence others, they are leading—with or without a "position." When part of your team, these people bring perspective and influence you'd likely never achieve on your own (Muhammad & Cruz, 2019).

Team Building

In his groundbreaking book *Diffusion of Innovations*, Everett M. Rogers (1962) describes how different types of people throughout an organization respond to change. Although his book is more than sixty years old, it still provides great insight into what organizations implementing change experience. Rogers (1962) writes that those we lead fall into five distinct categories based on their response to change: (1) innovators, (2) early adopters, (3) early majority, (4) late majority, and (5) laggards.

1. **Innovators:** Innovators are adventurous, comfortable with risk, and excited to try new things. Innovators are exciting for leaders, because they often give quick affirmation to leader decisions. However, they make up a very small part of a school (2.5 percent), and their eagerness to change has the potential to negatively impact their influence over others. Your leadership team will likely have innovators on it, but because of their small percentage,

they will likely be outnumbered. Innovators are great idea generators and dreamers. They are a great antidote for complacency but have limited influence because of their small numbers and fast-charging personalities.

2. **Early adopters:** Early adopters are influential and respected. They typically adopt change early but with a sense of caution and attention to detail. Early adopters (13.5 percent) are often thought leaders and influencers in a school. When I work to build a team of leaders, finding individuals in this group is a priority. While innovators are not too concerned with the risk of change, early adopters are very focused on the usefulness and potential of the change. Early adopters are great thought partners for leaders. They are often open-minded to change and have great influence over the all-important early majority. These individuals are often natural leaders. When they have questions, the questions likely represent the concerns of a group that looks to them for their leadership. When you form your team, early adopters will form the core because of their ability to support the leader and influence others.

3. **Early majority:** Those in the early majority adopt change only after they begin to see the success of early adopters. Rogers (1962) states that the remainder of the first half of a school belongs to the early majority (34 percent). While his percentages are by no means exact, it is important to recognize how our ability to share leadership with influential early adopters gives us influence over approximately half of our organization relatively early. That said, those in the early majority have a very strong place on your leadership team.

   Like the influential early adopters, early majority members are deliberate and careful in assessing change. They ask great questions, highlight possible misunderstandings, and help a leadership team to ensure the plan for change is well orchestrated and communicated. They have little excitement for change the way innovators do and are very focused on the practical usefulness of the change for them and the students they serve.

These first three groups will make up most of your shared leadership. Combined, they are innovative, influential, and deliberate and will help you to ensure the direction of your school is meaningful and practical. But what of the last two groups?

4. **Late majority:** The next group, the late majority (34 percent), will be the focus of your leadership's energy and influence. They will resist change initially and will likely require individual support to influence their change. This group is characterized by their skepticism and traditionalism. Due to

their numbers in the organization, they can often feel overwhelming to leaders. However, if you are intentional in sharing leadership and influence with the first three groups, you likely have already begun to see half of your school engaging in change.

Rogers (1962) suggests this group is resistant to change and typically only changes when there is enough organizational pressure for change that they realize they are in the minority. Remember, we still have the responsibility as leaders to make sure we adequately address the causes of rational resistance. The many leadership teams I have organized have featured a few, intentionally chosen late majority members. There will likely be some who have great influence on others. Depending on the personality of these individuals, they can provide support to your leadership team, but only in the right circumstances.

If you and your leadership team are new to leading together, be careful to not bring in a late majority member who could overpower the collective strength of your team. That said, if your team is established or the individuals are strong enough, it may be worth bringing the right late majority member onto your leadership team to gain perspective from one of those you are trying to reach. The late majority will change, but only once they feel the change has become widely accepted enough that they feel pressure to get on board or be left behind.

5. **Laggards:** Finally, laggards are most resistant to change and hold tightly to the way they have always done things, even when the rest of the school has adopted the change. The laggards (16 percent) will surface over time. As the direction of your school materializes, ownership increases, and the late majority begin to embrace change, you will often experience a "vocal minority." These individuals are not impossible to influence, but they are the group in which irrational resistance is most likely to occur. Laggards should not be part of your leadership team because they are generally typified by a great effort to resist change or new direction at all costs.

As noted in chapter 4 (page 67), all leaders make some of those they lead uncomfortable. If you have a team full of the right people and lead predictable change, as outlined in the previous chapter, laggards will be predictably uncomfortable. In my experience, this discomfort may cause them to be very vocal and resistant to change. However, I encourage you to ask yourself, "Are the right people uncomfortable?" If your laggards are uncomfortable, this is typically a symptom of successfully developing change. That never excuses us as leaders from treating them with respect and working to meet their needs, but we should not allow a vocal minority to have undue influence on our emotions or decisions.

Leaders who build a majority that adopts change can positively influence every member except the laggards.

How to Lead Your Leaders

Even with the right people on your team and clear goals for your work together, your leadership team still reflects your leadership. For some of us, sharing leadership is more natural than for others. Remember in my stories about becoming a new principal that it was not hard for me to share leadership because I didn't have the slightest clue what I was doing. When I became a high school principal and wore the pressure of somehow "replacing" my best friend, shared leadership wasn't my initial focus. When we surround ourselves with people whose talent and perspectives make us better leaders, we can't allow what qualified them for the position to feel threatening.

Instead, to be successful leading other talented leaders, we should be open-minded and vulnerable. Just being surrounded by talent is not enough. In fact, bringing in those who could make you better only to do it all yourself and deny them access to leadership will frustrate your leaders, invalidate the purpose of your team, and build others' frustration toward you (Fernandez & Velasquez, 2023).

Using Vulnerability as Connection Instead of Weakness

If I asked you to think about what makes a strong leader, what characteristics would come to mind? Traditionally, a commanding presence, an unwavering confidence, a firm handshake, and a directive style typify strong leaders. On the other hand, the ability to build relationships, communicate, care, and listen could be easily misunderstood as the opposite of strength (Dick, 2023). I have heard this in conversations about leaders who express not being good at the "touchy feely" stuff and just "want to get the job done."

Instead, the ability to make others feel safe enough to share constructive feedback is one of the greatest measures of strength in leaders. I have learned how precious honesty is, especially among those whose opinions I value most. I put great effort into relationships with those who care enough to share difficult things with me when I need to hear them. Without this feedback, it is easy to believe "no news is good news." In other words, many leaders feel that the absence of constructive feedback means that everyone supports the direction of the leader. Instead, in the absence of trust, staying quiet is more often a form of self-protection (Tourish, 2014).

Some of the stereotypical characteristics linked with strong leadership can cause separation between leaders and their staff. Confident, strong, and directive leaders often feel unapproachable to those they lead. However, transformational leaders are often known for their likability, approachability, respect for employees, transparency, and genuine concern for others' well-being (Kegan & Lahey, 2001). Transformational leadership requires trust and vulnerability.

Throughout this book, I have tried to practice vulnerability. My own successes, failures, celebrations, and losses are so much a part of my leadership that it is almost impossible not to share them. That said, vulnerability is almost always frightening. Even as I write this book, I likely will never know how readers receive it. Will my experiences resonate with readers? Will my heart come through in my writing? How will readers perceive me, especially my mistakes? These are questions I have had to push aside to muster the courage to lay out my professional life like an open book. It is natural to want to wait for others to show we can trust them before taking the leap of vulnerability. Quite frankly, we don't have that luxury as leaders. Vulnerability precedes trust.

Did you ever do a trust fall as a child? I will never forget standing atop a raised platform at summer camp with my heels dangling precariously over the edge and trying to push aside every logical fear my mind could produce long enough to fall backward into the arms of my fellow campers. I had seen them catch many other campers before me, but I was unquestionably the biggest. As I stood silently contemplating my eight-year-old life, I couldn't help but have doubts about some of the kids whose arms were the only thing between me and the ground. There were many reasons to not lean back, but I did . . . and I hit their arms, which barely budged, and took my place in line so the next camper could endure their own little slice of summer camp psychological torture.

As leaders, we are the ones on the platform. We build the team, share the goal, communicate the vision, and then lean back. It's only when our team catches us that the next member of the team is willing to trade places with us. When those we lead see our vulnerability, our willingness to welcome and engage in professional dissent for the purpose of improving, and our choice to not take feedback too personally, they are more willing to trust us to catch them when they are vulnerable. Vulnerability is scary, and I don't suggest throwing yourself from the platform into just anyone's arms; but if you have the right team and the right goals, you'll never experience the true power of shared leadership until you lean back.

Helping Others Win

One of the most fulfilling ways to transform shared leadership is to help others win. As we discussed in the previous chapter, each of us has unique strengths.

Tragically, many leaders spend considerable time and energy not excelling in their unique strengths but trying to outwork or overcompensate for their weaknesses. Instead, doesn't it just make more sense to find someone who is better than us and help that person win?

In the elementary school where I worked, my assistant principal was a mathematical genius. Numbers and systems just worked for her. Early on, our leadership team recognized a needed change to our master schedule. With their help, we created a wish list of what would help move the needle for teachers and students. When it came time to build a master schedule, though, it became abundantly clear that our assistant principal, Faith, was more skilled in designing it than I was. Sure, I could have built a schedule. It would have taken longer, wouldn't have been as good, and likely would've had multiple problems. Instead, I got out of the way of someone more talented than me and let Faith help us get better. However, just allowing her to build the initial draft of our schedule didn't help her win.

The new master schedule had things people loved and other things that some didn't like at all. I needed her intelligence to make our leadership better, but, in return, I could offer her the protection and support of my position. When it came time to share the draft schedule with others, I took the lead, not with her exciting innovations, but with the challenges and less exciting parts. As I explained these things, I was no doubt parroting what I heard her say. But as principal, I took the responsibility of sharing the hard part. Then I celebrated Faith's innovation and creativity. It was her creativity that made these things happen, but I had the power to shield and support her in becoming the master schedule guru. Of course, there was never a perfect schedule, but it was easier for her to lean into this task when she knew her work was recognized and celebrated and she wouldn't be alone to deliver the hard parts.

When our people win, we win. Unfortunately, self-doubt can cause us to miss opportunities to multiply the genius of others by expecting ourselves to have all the answers. We can stop trying to *be* the best at everything and instead *find* those who are the best at a few things. When we find someone with complimentary gifts, we have a responsibility to multiply that person for the betterment of our school.

In her book *Multipliers*, Liz Wiseman (2017) explains five characteristics that separate leaders who multiply talent from those who diminish it. First, multiplying leaders are *talent magnets*. They attract, seek, and optimize the talents of others while giving them intentional opportunities to shine. They are also *liberators*. Through reflection and vulnerability, multiplying leaders create safety in the work environment that gives others the security to speak up and share their opinions. Multiplying leaders are *motivators*. They set high expectations and challenge those around them toward meaningful goals where they can achieve more than they ever thought possible. In their vulnerability, multiplying leaders are *debaters*. They encourage diverse perspectives and expect those around them to respectfully question the status quo in pursuit of greatness. Finally, these leaders are *investors*. They don't find talent only to control it. They grow it, encourage it, and release it. They find greatness in others and unleash them in their school to be the best (Wiseman, 2017). Leaders who take this approach will experience great success because those around them are experiencing great success.

Now, stop and reflect on your experiences with sharing leadership. Record your thoughts in a notebook or journal.

> **Stop and Reflect: Are You Sharing Leadership? If So, How? Do You Have the Right Team With a Clear Focus?**
>
> With whom are you sharing leadership? Have you found the right people with the right skills and influence to contribute to your leadership? If so, do these people understand their purpose as leaders in the school?
>
> Take a moment to reflect on those leading with you or those who could be part of that team. How is their leadership making your school better? How are they making *you* better as a leader? Are you multiplying them to help them be their very best, or are you working incredibly hard at things they will naturally be better at than you?
>
> Record your thoughts before you continue reading.

Strategies to Build Shared Leadership

Building shared leadership begins with you. Unfortunately, leaders miss this all the time. Their leadership teams are formed by title or election instead of careful consideration of what leaders need to be great. One common example of a leadership team formed by title is a team comprised only of department chairs whose title is solely based on years of experience. I'm not saying department chairs shouldn't be on your leadership team, only that being a department chair shouldn't be the only qualifying criteria. In chapter 3 (page 51), I asked you to consider your leadership style. This is a great place to begin when thinking about sharing leadership. The primary goal in sharing leadership is not to surround yourself with people who agree with you or look and sound like you. Instead, you should be looking for people who will help make your leadership something different than it would be on your own.

The following strategies will help you form a leadership team that focuses on everyone's unique strengths and ability to contribute.

Determine Your Strengths and Areas of Need

Chapter 3 (page 51) focused on knowing and becoming the leader you aspire to be. The reason this chapter precedes the topic of sharing leadership is that the most effective shared leadership helps us to be what we wouldn't be on our own. When you consider those who can help multiply your leadership in your school or district, you will find many skill sets as unique to your own. As I shared in chapter 3, Faith, my assistant principal, offered incredible strengths she could bring to my leadership, and we experienced a shared impact I could have never realized on my own. As you think about people in your organization, consider how you might recognize and recruit talent to multiply your leadership.

Include People Who Are Approachable, Credible, and Aspirational

Consider the three leadership styles discussed in chapter 3—approachable, credible, and aspirational. Which one best describes your unique contribution to your school? You likely are pretty good at more than one of these, but I encourage you to focus on the area where you naturally excel. With your strength in mind, who in your organization could you recruit who is truly effective in the other two areas?

As a new principal, I could build relationships, but I didn't have credibility in instruction or content. I needed credibility and inspiration. On our leadership team, we had great young teachers, beloved veteran teachers, and instructional coaches. Their individual influence was so profound that collectively, we had the unique ability to empower and inspire. They would have never said they were inspirational, but they clearly inspired their colleagues because they believed what they said. You need all three leadership styles on your team.

Include Innovators, Early Adopters, and Early Majority Members

Surround yourself with a mix of innovators, early adopters, and early majority individuals. You want those who are fearless and excited for change, but you especially want those who will influence their peers. You also need people who are constructively skeptical. These are not the individuals who are trying to find problems to avoid change at all costs, but they will help you and your innovators anticipate the rational concerns of those throughout campus who initially resist.

Each person on your team offers a unique combination of skills. You may have an inspirational innovator who excites people but whose influence would wane over time without the help of a more credible early majority. You could also have a credible early majority member who is known for their output and isn't afraid to ask hard questions before committing to change. Remember, you are gathering skills and influence to build a collective leadership beyond what you could ever have alone.

Consider Whom Your Leadership Team Represents

Consider whom your leadership team represents. Unfortunately, most schools don't consider this from the beginning. As I noted at the beginning of this section, department chairs are often the easiest choice for high schools. Department chairs may make great team members but might not represent all the teachers they serve. If a department chair teaches only AP calculus throughout the day, a ninth-grade algebra 1 teacher may not see them as someone who speaks on their behalf. Another example is your specialized staff. A leadership team full of core content teachers will have a hard time speaking on behalf of extracurricular teachers or paraprofessionals.

Begin with your needs and the collective leadership style of your team. However, once these needs are met, ensuring adequate representation avoids isolating certain staff members who may already be prone to feeling left out.

Figure 5.1 offers a tool you can use when building your leadership team. It begins with *you*. Jot down notes about your leadership style, approach to change, and who you influence. Then use the rest of the chart to start building a complete leadership team by style and influence that represents your school by spreading your collective influence.

Leadership Team Member	Leadership Style *Does this person influence others through approachability, credibility, or aspiration?*	Approach to Change *Is this person an innovator, early adopter, or part of the early majority?*	Who They Influence *Over whom does this person have the greatest influence? Whom do they represent?*

Figure 5.1: Leadership team formation tool.

*Visit **go.SolutionTree.com/educatorwellness** for a free reproducible version of this figure.*

Establish Priorities for Your Leadership Team

With your team taking shape, it is time to focus on your team's work. However, after an entire chapter focused on leading change, remember that change for the sake of change is frustrating and unfruitful. You cannot possibly know where you want to go without knowing where you are. Every school has a culture. Some schools are intentional in building it, while others allow it to happen on its own. The first step in building culture for a leadership team is laying the foundation. Your school may not rise to every expected goal you set, but you also will not fall farther than the foundation of your culture. In other words, if your school or district is not clear on who you are or what you believe, there is no limit to how far you can fall.

In *Learning by Doing*, Richard DuFour, Rebecca DuFour, Robert Eaker, Thomas W. Many, Mike Mattos, and Anthony Muhammad (2024) refer to the foundation beneath an organizational floor as the four pillars—*mission*, *vision*, *values*, and *goals*. Once we define our purpose (mission), we can begin to ask ourselves if our behaviors match this purpose (values). With clarity of our compelling future (vision), we can begin to create a bread-crumb trail (goals) from our current reality to the future we envision (Vander Els & Ray, 2024).

Figure 5.2 (page 106) offers questions you can use to form your leadership team and establish these four pillars. By regularly returning to these questions, your leadership team will have a purposeful approach to building school culture.

Deploy Others in Their Strengths

With the right people, an honest view of your reality, and clarity of purpose and vision, your job as leader becomes more focused. You don't have to paint the picture; you just ready the palette. With your team, consider your goals, assess your current reality, learn together, consider the skills of those around you, and deploy leadership team members to move the school forward. For example, if you want to improve instruction, gather data to determine your current reality, choose a focus, learn best practices and successful instructional techniques working in your school, determine who on your team has the most credibility and influence in this area, and send them out to help others get better. You can replicate this cycle again and again, as shown in figure 5.3 (page 107).

There are a couple of simple nuances to this cycle worth reiterating. These elements become the steps your leadership team follow over and over throughout the year. The work of the leadership team crosses the divide between your current reality and your desired future. Schools don't change because it's flashy, because the district next to them is changing, or because of the promise of a new curriculum company.

Questions to Consider
Leadership:
• Does your school have a guiding coalition or leadership team?
• Is this team made up of a carefully chosen group of people who complement the leadership style and multiply the influence of their leader?
• Are any parts of your campus not adequately represented by the members of your team?
• Has this team taken the time to honestly evaluate the current reality of your campus?
Mission:
• Has your guiding coalition or leadership team discussed why your school exists?
• Is there a purpose for your school that unifies and focuses all professionals?
• Does your school ensure learning for all students?
Vision:
• Is there a compelling future for your school that provides motivation and meaning for your daily work?
• Have you looked at your school through the eyes of other stakeholders (students, families, and community members)?
• Does the school you hope to become motivate families and community members to want to take part in realizing this goal?
Values (Collective Commitments):
• Does your school confront toxic behaviors and those who are irrational in their resistance?
• Do you reflect on locations or settings within your school where the behaviors of staff don't align with who you want to be?
• Are members of the guiding coalition or leadership team clear on what their responsibility is in holding each other and others accountable?
• Does your school have an explicit list of behaviors that, when practiced, will move your school from your current reality to the purpose defined in your mission?
Goals:
• Does your school have goals that act like a "bread-crumb trail" between your current reality and the school you envision?
• Do your goals balance academic achievement, growth, and the processes of teams?
• Do you have specific times throughout the school year that leaders and teams reflect on their progress toward their goals?

Source: Adapted from Vander Els & Ray, 2024.

Figure 5.2: Four pillars reflection tool.

*Visit **go.SolutionTree.com/educatorwellness** for a free reproducible version of this figure.*

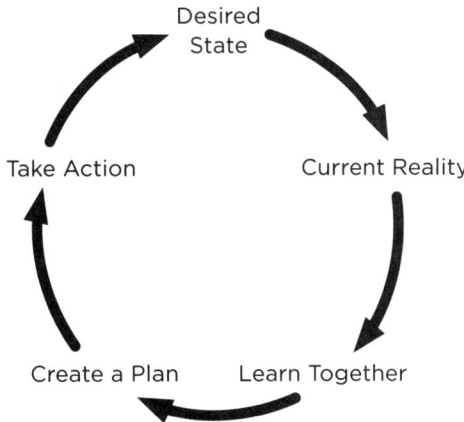

Figure 5.3: Leadership team function cycle.

Schools change when they see a discrepancy between who they are and who they aspire to become. Your team should always be considering your four pillars and searching for areas within the school culture that can be adjusted to bring you more in line with the school you aspire to become.

Now, stop and reflect on the kind of school you aspire to become, and what change might be needed to make this happen. Record your thoughts in a notebook or journal.

>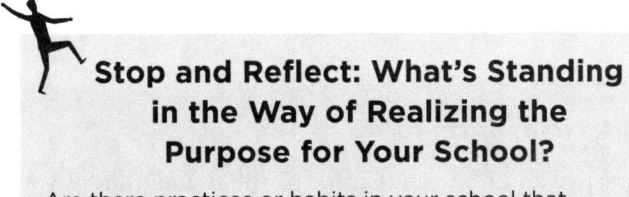
> **Stop and Reflect: What's Standing in the Way of Realizing the Purpose for Your School?**
>
> Are there practices or habits in your school that contradict the purpose of your school? Are there things standing in the way of the envisioned school you want for your students? Take a moment to consider areas where intentional change could improve your school.
>
> Record your thoughts before you continue reading.

When you find areas that need to be addressed, don't simply throw things against the wall and hope they stick. Utilize research and the practices of others to learn together. If your schedule needs adjustment, where can you find sample schedules to study together? If your assessment practices need improvement, where can you find research on best practices you could employ in your building?

Now, stop and reflect on what adjustments might be needed to implement change in your school (see page 108). Record your thoughts in a notebook or journal.

> **Stop and Reflect: Where Could You Go to Learn More about Implementing Change?**
>
> Where might you go to learn ways to address the adjustments needed to implement change? Are there schools you could learn from? Is there research you could study? Take a moment to plan how your team could learn more about this change.
>
> Record your thoughts before you continue reading.

With an area of growth highlighted and an approach chosen from research and best practice, your team takes action to improve. Remember to approach change intentionally, as outlined in chapter 4 (page 67), with the collective strength and influence of the entire leadership team.

With the right leadership team, you will have influence, innovation, creativity, representation, constructive questioning, and intentionality to meet the needs of your staff as we all work to be the best we can be for the students we serve. Just like a collaborative teacher team, the work of a leadership team is based around cycles of inquiry that proceed as follows.

1. Define your desired state.
2. Honestly assess your current reality.
3. Find best practice and research that forms the foundation of your plan.
4. Purposefully plan the use of your team's influence and the rollout of the change process.
5. Empathetically and intentionally lead change toward your desired state.

Now, stop and reflect on how to best utilize the unique strengths your leadership team offers to create change in your school. Record your thoughts in a notebook or journal.

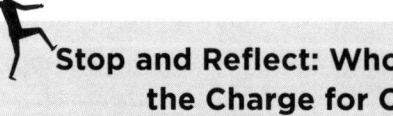

> **Stop and Reflect: Who Should Lead the Charge for Change?**
>
> Who should your team engage to help lead change? What leadership styles or change approaches would be most impactful? Plan how to deploy the unique strengths of your leaders to improve the change process for your school.
>
> Record your thoughts before you continue reading.

Conclusion

As a leader, there is no doubt you are talented, have a great heart, and work hard on behalf of those you lead. However, as you near the end of this book, I want to remind you of what has taken me years and a great deal of pain to learn. You are not enough. No matter how great, well-intended, or gifted, great leadership requires more than any single person can provide. Instead of trying to be your school's hero, you can only make leadership great when you share it.

That said, it is still *our* leadership. This means those you share it with should be carefully selected to make you better. With this team, a clear purpose, and the bravery needed to realize and examine your current reality, you will experience meaningful leadership unlike anything possible on your own. This is the promise of this book and the experience you and your school deserve.

EPILOGUE

Putting It All Together

While writing this book, it has been incredible to look back on the unlikely path my leadership has taken. I genuinely only ever wanted to help students fall in love with music the way I did as a young man. I could have never imagined I would move to a new district, become an administrator, make a best friend, become an elementary school principal, lead through massive change, see a campus transformed, lose my best friend, start all over again in his shadow, and relearn to share leadership.

Now, as an assistant superintendent, I work shoulder to shoulder with leaders who are trying to be their best for their campuses. While my story is pockmarked with ignorance, bullheadedness, loss, and fear, it brought me to this point. Hopefully, my story allows you to see what is possible. There is a path for you to greatness that won't cost you or the things you love most.

As I travel the world working with schools, no two leaders or organizations are the same. We all have our unique strengths and weaknesses and our own personal stories that have shaped us along the way. One thing is universal, though. Leadership matters, so you matter.

Know the Five Fundamental Truths of Leadership

Your journey will take you places mine never will, but for every one of us who leads in education, there are five fundamental truths that bind us. The beauty of these five truths, which I described in the five chapters of this book, lies in their ability to support us as human beings while making us better in our roles.

Balance Work and Life

We can't have leadership without a leader. Imbalance in educational leadership threatens the personal and professional lives of people every day. Imbalance shows no prejudice in who it ensnares. I've seen imbalanced leaders in every corner of North America, young and old, new and veteran, woman and man, in small systems and large. It is indiscriminate of race, culture, or tradition because it is intrinsic to the type of person who chooses a leadership role. That said, it's time to stop feeding the lie that greatness requires the sacrifice of the things that matter most to the person who assumes the role. Leaders deserve to be whole.

Make Time for Physical Wellness

I am more guilty than most at pretending I can continually ignore my most fundamental well-being in the pursuit of my goals. The job of educational leader is a big one, and no one is saying we should all set out to run a marathon. Still, the basics matter for your overall health and your ability to be your best. Don't shame yourself into invasive diets or massive, unsustainable shifts. Instead, make room to prioritize yourself, even if only just a little. Do not view sleep, hydration, and nutrition as luxuries. Instead, they should be a priority because they make you feel better and perform better. Leaders deserve to be well.

Be the Leader You Aspire to Be

There is more to leadership than putting out fires all day long. I'd be willing to bet you became a leader for something other than the chance to spend your day on your heels constantly responding to problems. Decide who you want to be and carve some time out of your day for this purpose. This is not selfish! Instead, it is a gift to you and your school. You are in the position you are in because of what you have to offer. Make sure that a profession fraught with hurry doesn't steal the unique impact you can offer teachers and students. Bring your best to your school instead of settling for professional survival. Leaders deserve to be focused.

Lead Change

Recognize that change is part of leadership. You can't avoid it, but you should handle it with intentionality and purpose. Education is a coordinated effort of giving, servant-hearted people. This means success in leading necessary change lies much less in your ability to lead the new direction than to lead the people. This doesn't mean change will be easy or that there won't be bumps along the way. However, just like your days spent in the classroom, you can apply your educational background to a "classroom" full of the adults you lead. In doing so, you will be more effective, connective, and respectful. Leaders deserve to change for the better.

Share Leadership

Finally, we all need a posse. This book and these five truths start with us individually and build out. There are things you can focus on as a leader to protect, preserve, and improve yourself, but then there are simply some areas where others will be better than you will. That's not just OK; it's one of the best parts of being a leader. Sharing leadership is exciting, fulfilling, and incredibly fun because it allows you to help others see and experience things within themselves they may have never known. Leaders deserve the strength of a team.

Share Your Story

My last hope for you is that, like me, you would be willing to share your story. I promise, it was not always easy sharing the stories you have read about my life throughout this book. However, the vulnerability it takes to share the fear, pain, and failure interwoven throughout my story comes with the blessing of helping others and honoring those who have helped me.

Leadership roles can be lonely, and it will always be difficult for those who have never walked in your shoes to completely understand. Maybe this is why some of my most joyous moments have come in laughing at my goofy mistakes with another leader or when I've realized that the bumps and bruises of my own experiences helped someone else. It's a blessing to be able to use your stories to encourage and empower others. After all, every leader deserves to experience professional greatness without compromising what matters most.

If you were to visit the quaint little town where I worked, you'd notice the back of the scoreboard at the end of the high school football field. Facing the campus is a two-stories-tall sign that reads, "It's not about me, it's about the G." These were the words Aaron shared with a student body and staff who had just erupted to his announcement as their new high school principal only weeks before he passed. The "G" he referred to stood for Greenwood, our hometown and local school district.

In the months after his passing, this humble quote became synonymous with the legacy of a man no one could believe was gone. Today, his words have become the unofficial slogan of an entire school district, representing the strength of their collective impact for students. I have T-shirts, wristbands, and even a picture on the wall of my office that feature this quote. However, it wasn't until I wrote this book that I realized Aaron's quote, as meaningful as it is, just isn't true. Thousands of lives were touched, not by Aaron's commitment to his job or district, but by his commitment to who he was.

Over the course of this book, you've learned very little about Aaron's leadership style or his professional accomplishments. You don't know about his degrees, his certifications, or his many awards as a leader. The reason for this is simple but profound. None of that matters now. Aaron's legacy is not as a principal; it is as a man. He is remembered for the husband and father he was, for the son he was to his mother, for the selfless servant he was at his local church, and for the way he cared for everyone around him.

In the days following his passing, very few people told stories about Aaron the principal. Instead, they told stories about how he listened to them; how he and his wife brought food to their house during hard times; or how, no matter how busy he was, he always made them feel like the most important person in the world.

What you do matters so much. Your job is important and meaningful. However, the difficult truth, honestly, is that the day you move on to something else, your school will move on, too. Eventually, your professional legacy will be little more than a block in the foundation of the school or district where you served. On the other hand, as my career has progressed, I have learned the things that were first to go when I continually pushed myself to the limits were most important all along. It is my sincere hope that you will settle for nothing less than the best not just for your school but for *you*.

As my friend Maria Nielsen once told me, "When you leave your job, they're not going to build you a statue, but you want your children to invite you to their wedding" (M. Nielsen, personal communication, June 3, 2022). Those you lead deserve your best. Those you love deserve your best. Most importantly, you deserve your best. So, go be great, be whole, and change lives for the better.

References and Resources

Achor, S. (2010). *The happiness advantage: The seven principles of positive psychology that fuel success and performance at work.* New York: Broadway Books.

ACS Axial. (2023, November 15). *The harmful effects of sleep deprivation.* Accessed at https://axial.acs.org/biology-and-biological-chemistry/the-harmful-effects-of-sleep-deprivation on August 13, 2024.

Bass, B. M., & Riggio, R. E. (2006). *Transformational leadership* (2nd ed.). New York: Lawrence Erlbaum Associates.

Bolman, L. G., & Deal, T. E. (2021). *Reframing organizations: Artistry, choice, and leadership* (7th ed.). San Francisco: Jossey-Bass.

Boogren, T. H. (2020). *180 days of self-care for busy educators.* Bloomington, IN: Solution Tree Press.

BrainFirst Institute. (2024, April 22). *Our psychological need to feel competent at work, and the impact on motivation, engagement, and performance.* Accessed at www.brainfirstinstitute.com/blog/our-psychological-need-to-feel-competent-at-work-and-the-impact-on-motivation-engagement-and-performance on March 17, 2025.

Clear, J. (n.d.). *How to be more productive and eliminate time wasting activities by using the "Eisenhower Box"* [Blog post]. Accessed at https://jamesclear.com/eisenhower-box on August 12, 2024.

Clear, J. (2018). *Atomic habits: Tiny changes, remarkable results—An easy and proven way to build good habits and break bad ones.* New York: Avery.

Collins, J. (2001). *Good to great: Why some companies make the leap—and others don't.* New York: HarperBusiness.

Colten, H. R., & Altevogt, B. M. (Eds.). (2006). *Sleep disorders and sleep deprivation: An unmet public health problem.* Washington, DC: National Academies Press.

Covey, S. R. (1989). *The 7 habits of highly effective people.* New York: Simon & Schuster.

Dick, S. (2023). Weakness is the new strength: How vulnerability makes leaders stronger. *Transform, 1*(1). Accessed at https://digitalcommons.umassglobal.edu/cgi/viewcontent.cgi?article=1001&context=transform on August 12, 2024.

Duan, W., Ho, S. M. Y., Tang, X., Li, T., & Zhang, Y. (2014). Character strength-based intervention to promote satisfaction with life in the Chinese university context. *Journal of Happiness Studies, 15*(6), 1347–1361. https://doi.org/10.1007/s10902-013-9479-y

DuFour, R., DuFour, R., Eaker, R., Many, T. W., Mattos, M., & Muhammad, A. (2024). *Learning by doing: A handbook for Professional Learning Communities at Work* (4th ed.). Bloomington, IN: Solution Tree Press.

Duhigg, C. (2012). *The power of habit: Why we do what we do in life and business*. New York: Random House.

Eades, J. (2021, October 27). *Why great leaders share knowledge with their team (and the masses)* [Blog post]. Accessed at https://learnloft.com/2021/10/27/why-great-leaders-share-knowledge-with-their-team-and-the-masses on May 28, 2024.

Esposito, L. (2019, June 4). *Boundaries: A guide to making essential life decisions* [Blog post]. Accessed at www.psychologytoday.com/us/blog/anxiety-zen/201906/boundaries-guide-making-essential-life-decisions on March 13, 2024.

Fenn, K. (2023, August 20). *Can coffee or a nap make up for sleep deprivation? A psychologist explains why there's no substitute for shut-eye*. Accessed at https://medicalxpress.com/news/2023-08-coffee-nap-deprivation-psychologist-substitute.html on August 12, 2024.

Fernandez, J., & Velasquez, L. (2023, March 23). *Becoming more collaborative—When you like to be in control*. Accessed at https://hbr.org/2023/03/becoming-more-collaborative-when-you-like-to-be-in-control on August 12, 2024.

Fredrickson, B. L. (2001). The role of positive emotions in positive psychology: The broaden-and-build theory of positive emotions. *American Psychologist, 56*(3), 218–226.

Gavin, M. (2019, October 22). *3 common leadership styles and how to identify yours* [Blog post]. Accessed at https://online.hbs.edu/blog/post/styles-of-leadership on April 24, 2024.

Goel, N., Rao, H., Durmer, J. S., & Dinges, D. F. (2009). Neurocognitive consequences of sleep deprivation. *Seminars in Neurology, 29*(4), 320–339. http://dx.doi.org/10.1055/s-0029-1237117

Grandner, M. A. (2022). Sleep, health, and society. *Sleep Medicine Clinics, 17*(2), 117–139.

Greene, J. D. (2014). The cognitive neuroscience of moral judgment and decision making. In M. S. Gazzaniga & G. R. Mangun (Eds.), *The cognitive neurosciences* (5th ed., pp. 1013–1023). Cambridge, MA: MIT Press.

Greene, J. D., & Paxton, J. M. (2009, July 28). Patterns of neural activity associated with honest and dishonest moral decisions. *Proceedings of the National Academy of Sciences, 106*, 12506–12511. http://dx.doi.org/10.1073/pnas.0900152106

Greenleaf Center for Servant Leadership. (n.d.). *What is servant leadership?* Accessed at www.greenleaf.org/what-is-servant-leadership on August 12, 2024.

Haidt, J. (2006). *The happiness hypothesis: Finding modern truth in ancient wisdom.* New York: Basic Books.

Harvard Business Review Staff. (2004, January). *Leading by feel.* Accessed at https://hbr.org/2004/01/leading-by-feel on April 24, 2024.

Hoomans, J. (2015, March 20). 35,000 decisions: The great choices of strategic leaders. *Leading Edge Journal.* Accessed at https://go.roberts.edu/leadingedge/the-great-choices-of-strategic-leaders on September 13, 2024.

Hopkins, G. (2009, December 1). *Marriage, family, and the principalship: Making it all work—Part 1.* Accessed at www.educationworld.com/a_admin/admin/admin478_a.shtml on March 19, 2024.

Hunter, P. (2013, May 17). Your decisions are what you eat. *EMBO Reports, 14*(6), 505–508. http://dx.doi.org/10.1038/embor.2013.69

James, A. (2014). Work-life 'balance,' recession and the gendered limits to learning and innovation (or, why it pays employers to care). *Gender, Work & Organization, 21*(3), 273–294. http://dx.doi.org/10.1111/gwao.12037

Johnson, M. M. (2022). *Self-care is not enough! Educational Leadership, 79*(9), 68–73.

Judge, T. A., Bono, J. E., Ilies, R., & Gerhardt, M. W. (2002). Personality and leadership: A qualitative and quantitative review. *Journal of Applied Psychology, 87*(4), 765–780.

Kahneman, D. (2011). *Thinking, fast and slow.* New York: Farrar, Straus and Giroux.

Kanold, T. D., & Boogren, T. H. (2022). *Educator wellness: A guide for sustaining physical, mental, emotional, and social well-being.* Bloomington, IN: Solution Tree Press.

Kegan, R., & Lahey, L. (2001, November). *The real reason people won't change.* Accessed at https://hbr.org/2001/11/the-real-reason-people-wont-change on August 12, 2024.

Killingsworth, M. A., & Gilbert, D. T. (2010). A wandering mind is an unhappy mind. *Science, 330*(6006), 932.

Knoster, T. P., Villa, R. A., & Thousand, J. S. (2000). A framework for thinking about systems change. In R. A. Villa & J. S. Thousand (Eds.), *Restructuring for caring and effective education: Piecing the puzzle together* (2nd ed., pp. 93–128). Towson, MD: Brookes.

Liebowitz, D. D., & Porter, L. (2020). *Descriptive evidence on school leaders' prior professional experiences and instructional effectiveness.* Accessed at https://edworkingpapers.com/sites/default/files/ai20-260.pdf on August 12, 2024.

Lortie, D. C. (1975). *Schoolteacher: A sociological study.* Chicago: University of Chicago Press.

Lowrie, J., & Brownlow, H. (2020). The impact of sleep deprivation and alcohol on driving: A comparative study. *BMC Public Health, 20*(1), 980. https://doi.org/10.1186/s12889-020-09095-5

Luntz, F. (2007). *Words that work: It's not what you say, it's what people hear.* New York: Hyperion.

Lyubomirsky, S., King, L., & Diener, E. (2005). The benefits of frequent positive affect: Does happiness lead to success? *Psychological Bulletin, 131*(6), 803–855.

Maeda, T., Koga, H., Nonaka, T., & Higuchi, S. (2023). Effects of bathing-induced changes in body temperature on sleep. *Journal of Physiological Anthropology, 42*(1), 20.

Martin, T. L., & Rains, C. L. (2018). *Stronger together: Answering the questions of collaborative leadership.* Bloomington, IN: Solution Tree Press.

Mattos, M., Buffum, A., Malone, J., Cruz, L. F., Dimich, N., & Schuhl, S. (2025). *Taking action: A handbook for RTI at Work* (2nd ed.). Bloomington, IN: Solution Tree Press.

Meyers, M. C., & van Woerkom, M. (2017). Effects of a strengths intervention on general and work-related well-being: The mediating role of positive affect. *Journal of Happiness Studies, 18*(3), 671–689. https://doi.org/10.1007/s10902-016-9745-x

Muhammad, A. (2018). *Transforming school culture: How to overcome staff division* (2nd ed.). Bloomington, IN: Solution Tree Press.

Muhammad, A., & Cruz, L. F. (2019). *Time for change: Four essential skills for transformational school and district leaders.* Bloomington, IN: Solution Tree Press.

Ngwenya, B. N., & Utete, R. (2023). The impact of work-life balance on employee absenteeism: An empirical study. *International Journal of Development and Sustainability, 12*(9), 439–451.

Nishi, S. K., Babio, N., Paz-Graniel, I., Serra-Majem, L., Vioque, J., Fitó, M., et al. (2023). Water intake, hydration status and 2-year changes in cognitive performance: A prospective cohort study. *BMC Medicine, 21*(82).

Occupational Safety and Health Administration. (n.d.). *The cognitive effects of proper hydration.* Accessed at www.osha.gov/sites/default/files/2023Beat TheHeatWinners/Contest_Innovative_KentPrecision_CognitiveEffects Hydration.pdf on May 15, 2024.

Okamoto-Mizuno, K., & Mizuno, K. (2012). Effects of thermal environment on sleep and circadian rhythm. *Journal of Physiological Anthropology, 31*(1), 14. https://doi.org/10.1186/1880-6805-31-14

Psychology Today. (n.d.). *Imposter syndrome.* Accessed at www.psychologytoday.com/us/basics/imposter-syndrome on March 26, 2024.

Ray, J. (2019). *Crumbling foundations: The case for prioritizing self-care among educational leaders* [Doctoral dissertation, University of Arkansas]. ScholarWorks@UARK. https://scholarworks.uark.edu/etd/3275

Ray, J., Pijanowski, J., & Lasater, K. (2020). The self-care practices of school principals. *Journal of Educational Administration, 58*(4), 435–451.

Rock, D. (2008). SCARF: A brain-based model for collaborating with and influencing others. *NeuroLeadership Journal, 1,* 1–9.

Rogers, E. M. (1962). *Diffusion of innovations.* Glencoe, IL: Free Press of Glencoe.

ScienceDaily. (2023, September 6). *How sleep deprivation can harm the brain.* Accessed at www.sciencedaily.com/releases/2023/09/230906143429.htm on August 13, 2024.

Shiv, B., & Fedorikhin, A. (1999). Heart and mind in conflict: The interplay of affect and cognition in consumer decision making. *Journal of Consumer Research, 26*(3), 278–292.

Silvani, M. I., Werder, R., & Perret, C. (2022). The influence of blue light on sleep, performance and wellbeing in young adults: A systematic review. *Frontiers in Physiology, 13,* 943108. https://doi.org/10.3389/fphys.2022.943108

Tempesta, D., Couyoumdjian, A., Curcio, G., Moroni, F., Marzano, C., De Gennaro, L., & Ferrara, M. (2010). Lack of sleep affects the evaluation of emotional stimuli. *Brain Research Bulletin, 82,* 104–108. http://dx.doi.org/10.1016/j.brainresbull.2010.01.014

Tourish, D. (2014). Leadership, more or less? A processual, communication perspective on the role of agency in leadership theory. *Leadership, 10*(1), 79–98. https://doi.org/10.1177/1742715013509030

van Woerkom, M., Mostert, K., Els, C., Bakker, A. B., de Beer, L., & Rothmann, S., Jr. (2016). Strengths use and deficit correction in organizations: Development and validation of a questionnaire. *European Journal of Work and Organizational Psychology, 25*(6), 960–975. https://doi.org/10.1080/1359432X.2016.1193010

Vander Els, J. G., & Ray, J. (2024). *The foundation for change: Focusing on the four pillars of a PLC at Work*. Bloomington, IN: Solution Tree Press.

Velasquez, L., & Gleitsman, K. (2023, July 10). *6 ways to become a more collaborative leader*. Accessed at https://hbr.org/2023/07/6-ways-to-become-a-more-collaborative-leader on August 12, 2024.

Volonte. (2023, August 2). *Simplifying the Lippitt-Knoster model for managing complex change*. Accessed at www.volonte.co/insights/simplifying-the-lippitt-knoster-model-for-managing-complex-change on April 28, 2024.

Wang, D., Waldman, D. A., & Zhang, Z. (2014). A meta-analysis of shared leadership and team effectiveness. *Journal of Applied Psychology, 99*(2), 181–198. https://doi.org/10.1037/a0034531

Ward, M. E. S. (2018). *Strengths-based leadership experiences in child protection teams: A multiple case study* [Doctoral dissertation, Capella University]. ProQuest. www.proquest.com/openview/2e4925931fecfedf4435da40f691b35c/1?pq-origsite=gscholar&cbl=18750

Watson, P., Whale, A., Mears, S. A., Reyner, L. A., & Maughan, R. J. (2015). Mild hypohydration increases the frequency of driver errors during a prolonged, monotonous driving task. *Physiology and Behavior, 147*, 313–318. http://dx.doi.org/10.1016/j.physbeh.2015.04.028

Wiseman, L. (2017). *Multipliers: How the best leaders make everyone smarter* (Rev. and updated ed.). New York: HarperBusiness.

Yang, Y., & Raine, A. (2009). Prefrontal structural and functional brain imaging findings in antisocial, violent, and psychopathic individuals: A meta-analysis. *Psychiatry Research, 174*(2), 81–88. http://doi.org/10.1016/j.pscychresns.2009.03.012

Zaccaro, S. J. (2007). Trait-based perspectives of leadership. *American Psychologist, 62*(1), 6–16.

Index

A
absenteeism, 12
accountability, 25
   culture of, 79
   physical health and, 34–35
   practicing caring, 29–30
   structure for, 80–83
   Tier 1, 81, 82
   Tier 2, 81, 82–83
   Tier 3, 81, 83
   tiered pyramid of, 80–83
Achor, S., 21, 22
acknowledgment, 82–83
action plans, 74
affirmation
   motivation and, 57
   from selflessness, 18–19
anxiety
   imbalance and, 11–12
   resistance to change and, 87–89
   self-doubt and, 8–11
approachable leaders, 54, 57–58, 100, 103
aspirational leaders, 54–55, 103
authenticity, 54
authority
   accountability and, 81–83
   credibility and, 54
   shared leadership and, 96
autonomy, 78

B
balance, 7–30, 111–112. *See also* imbalance
   change leadership and, 69
   defining, 11
   elements of, 21–26
   intentional, 22–23
   pursuit of leadership and, 12–14
   stages of leadership imbalance and, 14–19
   strategies to find, 26–30
behavior
   building habits and, 24
   fear to behavior tool and, 21
   focus on in change efforts, 81–82
blue light exposure, 46
Bono, J. E., 53
Boogren, T. H., 35, 40–41, 44, 60
broaden-and-build theory, 21–22

C
caffeine, 32, 39–40, 48
calendars, 62–63
certainty, 77–78
change
   accountability structure and, 80–83
   action plans for, 74
   challenges of leading, 5
   consensus and, 72
   diagnosing, understanding, and addressing resistance to, 83–89
   difficulty of, 67–70
   effects of on individuals, 76–77
   incentives for, 73
   leader strength and, 70–71
   leading, 67–89, 112
   Lippitt-Knoster model for, 71–74
   messiness in, 3–4
   removing resistors to, 75
   resistance to, 67–70, 73, 74–80
   resources for, 73, 76
   SCARF model for, 77–79
   skills for, 73
   types of responders to, 97–99
   vision for, 72
check-ins, 83
cognition
   hydration and, 40–41
   nutrition and, 42
collaboration
   culture and, 83
   isolation and, 95–96
   leadership and, 53

Collins, J., 60
commitments, collective, 82
communication
 about limits, 24–25
 physical health and, 35
 sharing your story and, 113–114
 vulnerability and, 99–100
competence, 73
confidence, 100. *See also* imposter syndrome
 certainty and, 78
 credible leaders and, 54, 56–57, 58
 isolation and, 95
 leadership development and, 14
 self-doubt and, 3
 vulnerability and, 99–100
conflict, 3–4
consensus, 72–73
content knowledge, 19–20
continuous improvement, 70
Covid-19 pandemic, 33–34, 92
creativity, 22
credibility, 20, 75, 103
credible leaders, 54
Cruz, L. F., 74, 76, 79–80, 81, 96
culture, 79
 for change efforts, 83
 principals as keeper of, 83
 shared leadership and, 94

D

debators, 101–102
decision making, 22
 consensus in, 72
 hydration and, 39–41
 nutrition and, 42
 physical wellness and, 35–43
 sleep deprivation and, 38–39
deficiency mindset, 22–23, 52
dependency, on leaders, 12
Diffusion of Innovations (Rogers), 96–99
Dimich, N., 81
driving
 dehydration and, 40
 sleep deprivation and, 38
DuFour, R., 72, 105

E

Eades, J., 93–94
Eaker, R., 72, 105
early adopters, 97, 103–104
early majority, 97, 103–104
Educator Wellness (Kanold & Boogren), 44, 45
Eisenhower, D., 64–65
Eisenhower Box, 64–65
emotion
 change and, 68–69
 decision making and, 36–37
 hydration and, 40–41
 resistance to change and, 86–87
 sleep-deprivation and, 38
emotional intelligence, 54
empathy, 84–85, 86
empowerment, 54–55
engagement, 73
ethics, sleep deprivation and, 38–39
exercise, 47, 70, 71
expectations, 82, 83

F

failure, fear of, 12. *See also* fear
fairness, 79
faking it, 2–3
family life, 8, 10, 37–38
fear, 12
 behavior tool and, 21
 imbalance motivated by, 18–21
 resistance and, 80, 85–86
 self-sacrifice and, 17–19
 stages of imbalance and, 14–19
feedback, 95, 99, 100
 accountability and, 30
 personal and professional priorities tool and, 26–28
food habits, 33, 36, 41–43, 48–50
The Foundation for Change (Vander Els & Ray), 77, 94
four pillars, 105, 106
Fredrickson, B. L., 21–22

G

Gavin, M., 54, 56
Gerhardt, M. W., 53
Gilbert, D. T., 55–56
goals, 105, 106
 balancing professional and personal, 11
 intentionality and, 22–23
 for shared leadership, 105
 shared leadership and, 94–95
 time audits and, 63–65
Good to Great (Collins), 60
Greene, J., 36–37
Greenleaf, R. K., 17

H

Haidt, J., 37, 38
happiness
 decision making and, 37
 defining, 55–56
 hydration and, 40
 power of, 52–53
 success and, 21–22
The Happiness Advantage (Achor), 21
The Happiness Hypothesis (Haidt), 37
Harvard Business Review Staff, 54
health. *See* physical wellness

hedgehog concept, 60
heroic performance, 3, 93–94
Hopkins, G., 13–14
hydration, 36, 39–41, 48

I

Ilies, R., 53
imbalance
    defining, 11
    imposter syndrome and, 15–16
    motivation for, 18–26
    recognizing, 23–24
    sources of, 19–21
    stages of in leadership, 14–19
    unsustainable effort in, 16–18
importance, urgency vs., 64–65
imposter syndrome, 3, 4, 15–16, 19–20, 68, 94
    defining, 15
    leadership traits and, 53
incentives, for change, 73
innovators, 96–97, 103–104
intentionality, 22–23, 52–53
irrational resistance, 74–75, 79–80
isolation, 11–12, 18, 95–96
    leading change and, 80, 89

J

James, A., 11
journals and journaling, food, 42–43.
    See also reflection
Judge, T. A., 53

K

Kahneman, D., 42
Kanold, T. D., 35, 44, 60
Killingsworth, M. A., 55–56
Knoster, T., 71

L

laggards, 98–99
late majority, 97–98
leaders
    approachable, 54, 57–58, 100, 103
    aspirational, 54–55, 103
    credible, 54
    leading, 99–102
    who becomes, 12–14
leadership
    becoming the kind of leader you want to be, 3, 4–5
    for change, 67–89
    change and, 67–89, 112
    defining, 96
    discomfort and, 80
    faking it in, 2–4
    fundamental truths about, 3–4, 111–113
    growing strengths for, 51–65
    happiness and, 55–56
    how to lead leaders and, 99–102
    impact of on others, 56
    importance of, xiv–xv
    intentionality and, 22–23, 52–53
    job duty priorities in, 52–53, 59–60
    legacy and, 114
    motivation and, 57–59
    preparation for, 1–2, xiv–xv
    self-assessment of, 56–59
    servant, 17
    shared, 4, 5, 91–109, 112–113
    sharing stories about, 113–114
    stages of imbalance in, 14–19
    strength-based, 61
    time management and, 62–65
    time priorities and, 59–60
    traits and styles of, 53–55, 99–100, 102–103, 112
    who pursues educational, 12–14
    work–life balance and, 7–30
LearnLoft, 93–94
limits, communicating, 24–25
Lippitt, M., 71
Lippitt-Knoster model for change, 71–74, 76, 87–89
Lortie, D. C., 16

M

Malone, J., 81
Many, T. W., 72, 105
Martin, T. L., 53
Mattos, M., 72, 81, 105, xiii–xv
meaningful work, 114, xiii–xiv
messiness, 3–4
micromanaging, 69–70
mind wandering, 55–56
mindset
    deficiency, 22–23, 52
    imbalance and, 51–52
    nutrition and, 48–49
mission, 105, 106
modeling
    accountability, 29–30
    balance, 24–25
motivation. *See also* fear
    fear as, 18–19
    goals and, 94–95
    for imbalance, 19–21
    internal vs. external, 57
    job priorities and, 59–60
    leadership and, 57–59, 101–102
motivators, 101–102
Muhammad, A., 72, 74, 76, 79–80, 96, 105
Multipliers (Wiseman), 101–102
multiplying talent, 101–102

N

Nielsen, M., 114
nutrition, 33, 36, 41–43

O

open-mindedness, 99
overcompensation, 100–101
overwork, 7–10
    recognizing and admitting to, 23–24
    stages of imbalance and, 14–19
    unsustainability of, 16–18

P

partial sleep restriction, 38–39
Paxton, J., 36
peer support, 83
performance
    heroic leadership, 3
    hydration and, 40
    positive emotions and, 21–22
    shared leadership and, 91
    sleep deprivation and, 38, 39
    status, change, and, 77
perspectives
    on change, 79, 86
    feedback and, 27–28
    in shared leadership, 94, 95–96, 98–99, 102
physical wellness, 4, 31–50, 112
    decision making and, 35–43
    eating habits and, 33
    hydration and, 36, 39–41, 48
    imbalance and, 11–12
    nutrition and, 33, 36, 41–43, 48–50
    overview of, 32–35
    prioritizing, 43–45
    sleep and, 35, 37–39, 46–47
    strategies to improve, 45–50
physiological security, 34
positive psychology, 21–22
predictability, 76
presence, 55–56
priorities
    identifying and protecting, 28–29
    modeling balance and, 24–25
    personal and professional priorities tool for, 26–28
    physical wellness as, 43–45
    for shared leadership, 105
priority protection tool, 28–29
problem solving, dependency on leaders for, 12
productivity, 22
professional development, 1–2, xiv–xv
    anxiety and overwork in, 8–11
    educational leadership and, 12–13
    pain/discomfort in, 70–71
    strengths-based, 54–55, 61
protected time, 62–63

Psychology Today, 15
purpose, xiii–xiv
    change efforts and, 82
    goals and, 94–95
    happiness and, 22
    intentional effort and, 23–24
    leadership and, 12–13
    reflection on barriers to, 107

R

Rains. C. L., 53
rational resistance, 74–79
Ray, J., 32–34, 77, 82, 94
reflection
    on barriers to purpose, 107
    on the four pillars, 106
    on leadership in change, 108
    on leadership task priorities, 61
    on learning about change, 108
    on physical wellness, 44
    on resistance to change, 80
    on shared leadership, 102
    on your current level of balance, 26
relatedness, 78, 95–96
    vulnerability and, 99–100
relationships, 103
resentment, 24
resistance, 67–70, 73, 74–80
    diagnosing, understanding, and addressing, 83–89
    Lippitt-Knoster model for, 87–89
    SCARF model of, 77–79
    types of responders and, 98–99
resources, for change, 73, 76
Response to Intervention (RTI) at Work, 80–83
responsibility, individual, 34. *See also* accountability
Rock, D., 77, 84
Rogers, E. M., 96–99
roles
    burden of leadership, 3, 12
    defining leadership, 57
    isolation and, 113
    priorities and, 52
    shared leadership and, 92–94
routines
    hydration and, 48
    nighttime, sleep and, 47

S

safety, 86, 99–100, 101
    physiological, 34
SCARF model, 77–79, 84–87
Schoolteacher (Lortie), 16
Schuhl, S., 81
self-appraisal
    of leadership, 56–59
    physical health and, 35

of physical wellness, 44–45
of priorities, 28–29
of strengths and areas of need, 103–104
self-awareness, 22, 24
    leading change and, 69
    physical health and, 35
    tool for balance and, 26–28
self-care movement, 33–34
self-doubt, 3, 4
    anxiety and overwork due to, 7–10
    helping others win and, 101–102
    imposter syndrome and, 3, 4, 15–16, 19–20, 53, 68, 94
    stages of imbalance and, 14–19
self-image, 32
self-sacrifice, 8–11, 15, 18–19
servant leadership, 17
shared leadership, 4, 5, 91–109, 112–113
    defining, 94–95
    formation tool for, 104
    isolation and, 95–96
    overview of, 93–99
    priorities for, 105, 106
    strategies to build, 102–108
    strengths-based deployment for, 105, 107–108
    team building and, 96–99
    team function cycle for, 105, 107
skills, for change, 73
sleep, 36, 37–39
    strategies to improve, 46–47
snacks, 49–50
stability, 77–78
status, 77
stress
    change and, 69
    imbalance and, 11–12
Stronger Together (Martin & Rains), 53
styles, leadership, 54–59, 102–103
success, 95–96
    happiness and, 21–22
    helping others win and, 100–102
support, for change, 81–83, 86–87
    Lippitt-Knoster model for, 87–89
    SCARF model for, 83–87

T

Taking Action (Mattos, Buffum, Malone, Cruz, Dimich, & Schuhl), 81
talent, multiplying, 101–102
talent magnets, 101–102
teams
    building, 96–99
    cycles of inquiry in, 108
    function cycle of, 105, 107
    priorities for, 105
    shared leadership, 94
    who they represent, 104
Tier 1 supports, 81, 82
Tier 2 supports, 81, 82–83
Tier 3 supports, 81, 83
time and time management
    leadership and, 59–60
    for physical wellness, 34
    strategies for, 62–65
time audits, 63–65
Time for Change (Muhammad & Cruz), 74
tools
    fear to behavior, 21
    four pillars reflection, 106
    leadership style assessment, 58
    leadership tea, formation, 104
    Lippitt-Knoster systematic resistance assessment, 88
    personal and professional priorities, 26–28
    physical wellness self-rating, 45
    priority protection, 28–29
    SCARF individual resistance assessment, 84–85
    time audits, 63–65
Track Your Happiness app, 55–56
trait theory of leadership, 53–55
trust, 69–70, 100

U

unavailability, allowing, health, and, 46
urgency, 64–65

V

values, 105, 106
Vander Els, J. G., 77, 82, 94
vision, 54–55, 72, 105, 106
vulnerability, 3, 99–100, 113–114

W

Waldeman, D. A., 94
Wang, D., 94
warm bath effect, 47
weight management, 41–42
well-being, 2–4
    physical, 4, 31–50
    prioritizing sustainably, 4–5
    survey of educational leaders', 13–14
    work–life balance and, 7–30
wholeness, 4, 5
work ethic, 7, 15
work-life balance. *See* balance

Z

Zhang, Z., 94

The Principal's Backpack
Nancy Karlin Flynn
In *The Principal's Backpack*, Nancy Karlin Flynn draws on her background as a hiker and her years of experience leading schools to provide concrete ideas and practical tips on how to not only survive but thrive as a school leader.
BKG117

Benches in the Bathroom
Evisha Ford
Benches in the Bathroom offers K–12 leadership a wealth of field-tested, research-supported guidance to construct a school culture that values teacher contributions, operates on a framework of emotional wellness, and implements trauma-compassionate organizational strategies to ensure educator success and well-being.
BKG094

180 Days of Self-Care for Busy Educators
Tina H. Boogren
Rely on *180 Days of Self-Care for Busy Educators* to help you lead a happier, healthier, more fulfilled life inside and outside of the classroom. With Tina H. Boogren's guidance, you will work through thirty-six weeks of self-care strategies during the school year.
BKF920

Beyond Self-Care
Gail Markin
Explore the importance of well-being at individual, group, and system levels, as well as the role of leadership in supporting school cultures of well-being. Using research-based practices and excerpts of conversations from working educators, Markin delivers a guidebook to healthier, more passionate schools.
BKG079

Visit SolutionTree.com or call 800.733.6786 to order.

We don't just help schools make a change, we help them *be* the change

REAL IMPACT. RELEVANT SOLUTIONS. RESULTS-DRIVEN APPROACH.

From funding to faculty retention, the evolving demands schools face can be overwhelming. That's where we come in. With professional development rooted in decades of research and delivered by many of the educators who literally wrote the book on it, we empower schools to achieve meaningful change with real, sustainable results.

The change starts here. We can make it happen together.

 See how we can get real results for your school or district.

Scan the code or visit:

SolutionTree.com/Results-Driven

 Solution Tree

LET'S SEE WHAT **WE CAN** DO TOGETHER